Winning the Generation Wars at Work:

Making (**Your**) Age An Asset

MERRY BROWN

Additional books by Merry Brown

Non-fiction
How to Be Unprofessional at Work: Tips to Ensure Failure
*The Food Addict: Recovering from Binge Eating Disorder
     & Making Peace with Food*

Fiction
<u>The Four Families Series</u>
Gold Manor Ghost House
Crimson Hall Ghost House
Silver Tree Ghost House
Rose Star Ghost House

<u>The Exiled Trilogy</u>
The Knowers
The Second Fall
The United

YA Books Imprint
ISBN: 978-0-9899934-9-4
January 2026

Front cover designed by Merry Brown using Canva.

This book is dedicated to:

Eleanor Roosevelt, American First Lady and chair of the Universal Declaration of Human Rights drafting Committee

"It isn't enough to talk about peace. One must believe in it. And it isn't enough to believe in it. One must work at it."[1]

and

St. Maximillan Kolby, who volunteered to die in place of another in the German death camp of Auschwitz

"No one in the world can change Truth. What we can do and should do is to seek truth and to serve it when we have found it. The real conflict is the inner conflict. Beyond armies of occupation and the hecatombs [e.g. the sacrifice of many victims] of extermination camps, there are two irreconcilable enemies in the depth of every soul: good and evil, sin and love. And what use are the victories on the battlefield if we ourselves are defeated in our innermost personal selves?"[2]

Table of Contents

Prologue: Meditation on War

People and nations go to war due to failure. Failure to communicate. Failure to hold and enforce basic standards. Failure to treat others with dignity and respect.

War is an astronomical waste of resources. But the greatest price is the human cost: physical, emotional maiming, generational trauma, and death. So much senseless loss!

Let's suppose you decide to go to war at work. Have you counted the costs? Can you afford this financially? Morally, can you bear the brunt of treating other people cruelly?

We are morally and financially obligated at work to actively bring about the opposite of war: peace.

Peace is not simply achieved because we want it. Peace takes sustained, intentional effort. It takes noticing when things are not working and addressing them sooner rather than later, so issues don't fester and spread like poison.

If you are 'at war' with other generations or anyone at work, stop and consider:

- What is your endgame?
- What resources, human and financial, are **you** going to have to burn through to achieve **your** goal?

If your goal is to attract and retain talent, lead innovation, provide excellent customer service, inspire a healthy work environment, stay in business, and make money then you need diversity of thought and experience from all generations. Eliminating generations from your work pool is foolish... and illegal.

If you want to win in the marketplace of today and beyond, put down your verbal weapons and dismantle the arsenal of derogatory thoughts you have about people in different generations, and get to work building a resilient, engaged, and high performing work force through the practice of consistent curious dialogue.

Introduction

'Nobody wants to work anymore,' is a resounding refrain heard from all corners of the working world. The work ethic of the younger generation is constantly called into question, usually accompanied by a shaking head and voice dripping with derision.

'You can't open a pdf,' is code for calling older generations in the workplace out of touch. *They* don't know how things work. *They* are largely oblivious and are a liability to running a successful and humane business in 2025 and beyond, because *they* do not understand how things work today.

The generational divide is nothing new. It's reminiscent of the differences in pop culture. "This isn't real music!" says almost every dad to his child for the past 100 years.

While the generational gaps at work are nothing completely new, the world of work we currently inhabit is so startlingly different from the world of work since the dawn of time, the fact that it's not more dysfunctional is a wonder.

To the generational divides that cause so much stress, loss of productivity, revenue, and heartache, I propose a straightforward, eminently doable solution that I will walk you through in chapter one.

While this book is about addressing generational differences, and while there are real differences, there is much more that unites us.

We are all human and have basic human needs. We all have needs for connections, community, to be cared for and to care for others, to be seen as competent, respected, and loved.

Consider Maslow's Hierarchy of Needs.

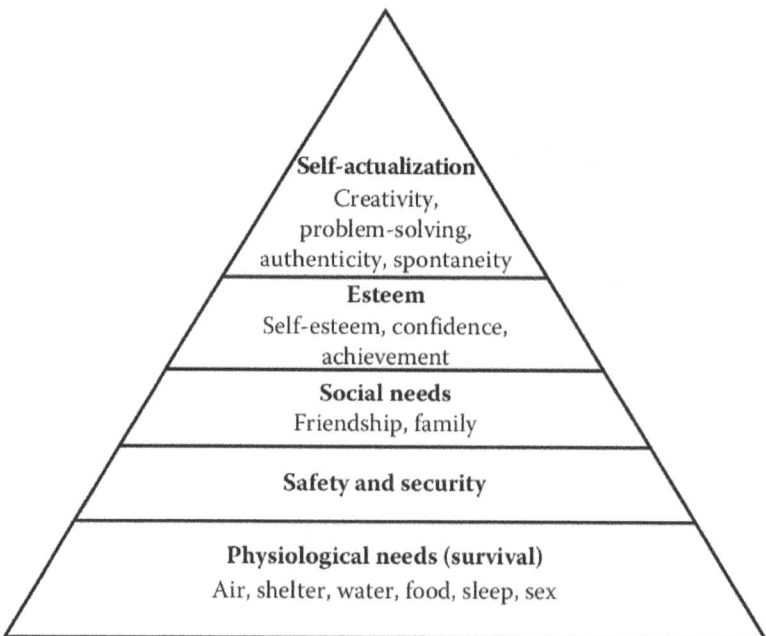

Self-actualization
Creativity,
problem-solving,
authenticity, spontaneity

Esteem
Self-esteem, confidence,
achievement

Social needs
Friendship, family

Safety and security

Physiological needs (survival)
Air, shelter, water, food, sleep, sex

We all have needs we are trying to meet. To address generational differences, it is important to see just how much we are alike as humans, so we don't fall prey to thinking that our colleagues from other generations are completely other, unknowable, and therefore unreachable.

We can all, at any moment, experience:

- Being shunned or embraced
- Betrayal or faithfulness
- Death or birth of a loved one
- Decline in health or healing
- Financial ruin or win-fall
- Great disappointment or satisfaction
- Job loss or opportunity
- Tragedy or joy

We are all part of the human community with its many highs, lows, and the average every day. We can choose to 'other' someone based on a difference or embrace and value the difference.

The poisonous idea that the generation gaps at work are unbridgeable gulfs permeates the air we breathe. And so we talk about generational divides and wars. War always 'others,' making it easier to mistreat whomever we've decided to label 'they.' This is the wrong way to go.

Instead of being at war with our colleagues, let's really win. What does really winning look like? Really winning is you and me, working together for a common goal where we have our needs met. If we conceive of winning as 'I win over you,' then we are doomed from the very start.

It is unrealistic to think you will have a high performing, engaged, collaborative, and healthy work environment where colleagues are pitted against each other in a war of generational wills.

Really winning at work involves understanding and being converted to the truth that people are communal by nature. We need each other to achieve both our personal and collective (business) goals.

Therefore, let's address these differences. Let's look at them. Let's find the path forward that chooses a different narrative, away from the story that people in different generations are 'bad' and suspect in some fundamental way and towards the fruitful narrative that this difference is an opportunity for greatness, health, and innovation that ought not be squandered.

Section I: The Antidote to the Generation Wars at Work

Chapter 1: The Antidote

You picked up this book because you want to know the answer to the following questions:

How do I work with these older/younger people who are so different from me?

How do I get them to see they are (check all that apply):

    ___ Entitled

    ___ Irrelevant

    ___ Have a poor work ethic

    ___ Out of touch

    ___ Unprofessional

How do I get them to change?

While we're at it, why am I the one who must put up with this behavior? We're at work, so they should pull themselves together!

I hear your frustration. Luckily, you're in the right place to find the answers to these questions. But I must first prepare you, because the answer is at the same time simple and very difficult. I want to set your expectations for the antidote to the culture wars. It's not easy, and it's not quick. This antidote doesn't take the form of a one-time shot. It's a medicine that you must take every day for the rest of your life. I am not kidding, and this is not hyperbole.

The antidote to the generation wars at work is DIALOGUE.

Real Dialogue.

Ongoing Dialogue.

Having A Dialogue Mindset.

Dialogue is the antidote to unnecessary and unmanaged conflict.

You may be skeptical. How could dialogue be the answer? That's a reasonable response. Let's go on this journey together to find out.

Chapter 2: What a Dialogue Is

A Real Dialogue is a particular form of conversation. It is a process in which an idea or issue is brought forward to be investigated. My idea/issue and your counter idea/perspective give way to the synthesis (which is ours).

This synthesis does not necessarily mean we walk away from a dialogue agreeing with each other, but we do leave changed. We are changed because of the experience we've had in giving and receiving information.

An understanding one forms when we are present, engaged, and listening to one another. Communication, especially when we're talking about what's important to us, is expressed in our body language and tone, just as much, if not more, than in the words themselves.

Ideally, a dialogue takes place between a few people who have come prepared to listen, learn, and move forward. While we can, and should, engage in group conversations, we should not trick ourselves into believing that the dynamics of a dialogue don't change with each person added. The more people present in a conversation, the easier it is to not hear from all of the voices present.[3]

Through the process of dialogue, we practice:

- Listening to understand

- Articulating our thoughts and ideas
- Curiosity and charity
- Respect for our colleagues
- Engagement in the process

Listening to understand

When you think about a dialogue, what comes to mind? Is it your chance to tell the other person what you think while tapping your foot as they respond and you 'listen,' but in reality you are just waiting them out so you can start talking again?

Engaging in dialogue means that we need to listen as much, or more, than we speak. What you say next has everything to do with what the other party just said. The better you are at listening to what the others in the dialogue are saying, how they are saying it, and what is left unsaid, the more information you'll have to move the conversation forward.

Dialogue where the parties are present and engaged can lift us out of the same old story we've been telling ourselves, **because now we have new information**. And with this new information, we can revisit where we started and see our starting place was possibly based on the limited information we had available. And since the dialogue presents us with new information, we can amend where we started from and move forward.

Clearly articulate your thoughts and ideas

Fruitful dialogue requires clarity. To engage with a colleague about a problem or situation, such as office norms, project standards, or resource allocation, we need to know what the issues are for us. Instead of, 'this is a mess,' 'she is disrespectful,' 'this place is toxic,' or 'we should be going in a different direction,' be specific and clear in your mind.

Instead of saying, "this is a mess," be able to articulate:

- What specifically is a mess?
- Why do you think it is a mess?
- What, specifically, might be happening if it was well ordered and running smoothly?

Instead of saying, "she is disrespectful," articulate:

- What specific behaviors she is (or isn't) doing that fall under the title *disrespectful*?
- What would respectful behavior look like instead?

Instead of saying, "this place is toxic," articulate:

- What specifically is toxic in your workspace?
- What parts of work aren't toxic?
- What (specifically and realistically) needs to change to have a healthy work environment?

Instead of saying, "we should be going in a different direction," articulate what you mean:

- In what specific direction is the team headed? Why do you think this is the case?
- In what direction do you think the team should be headed?
- Why is this direction preferable?

Curiosity and charity

Articulating your thoughts and ideas takes self-reflection and curiosity. What do I really think and why do I think it?

While a fruitful dialogue takes internal curiosity, it also requires us to be genuinely curious about what our conversation partners want and need. A real dialogue requires we divest ourselves of the false belief that we know why the other person is doing/thinking what they are doing/thinking.

Prior to a dialogue, we take educated guesses at what other people see, want, and need, but it is only a guess. It is in the process of the dialogue that we get more information, so we can see what's really going on. This is vital information for successful collaboration.

However, we are unlikely to be curious when we have no charity for the persons we are talking with. The principle of charity states we give others the benefit of doubt. When people misspeak or misstep, instead of immediately assigning negative motives to the action, we pause, take a step back, and ask for clarification.

Operating with the principle of charity in mind means we want the good for ourselves and the other. Imagine trying to engage in a real dialogue where you feel others have it in for you, their hostility rolling off in waves? Without feeling a level of goodwill emanating from your conversation partner, real dialogue dies before it begins.[4]

Respect for colleagues

If you don't respect your colleagues, it's hard to want to engage in the process of real dialogue. It's hard to fake respect, and there are many legitimate reasons we may lack respect for our colleagues.

Luckily for us, respect can be understood in a variety of ways. There is the kind of respect that is earned and lost due to the actions we take or don't take. This is **not** the kind of respect I'm talking about. Rather, the type of respect I'm referring to here is the baseline respect that is owed to all people simply because they are members of the human community.[5]

While we must respect our conversation partners to have a real dialogue, respect must be reciprocal. If someone is treating you disrespectfully, real dialogue won't happen.

It is important to be mindful about what disrespect is. It may feel bad or uncomfortable to be disagreed with, or for someone to have a version of an event that differs from yours. The bare fact of disagreement does not mean you are being disrespected. We must mind our own reactions and not jump to conclusions that we are being treated disrespectfully **simply due** to the other person's point of view, tone of voice, conflict style, or personality.

Engagement in the process

A real dialogue is active. It requires being present, thinking, listening, refining, and imagining. It means being open to the process, because the magic is found in the process. There is no way around. The only way through is through.

Through the process of dialogue, new possibilities emerge. Space is made to move from positions to needs, making room for the Third Way.

This Third Way involves turning the generation wars away from losing and toward opportunity, engagement, innovation, and flourishing working environments for all the members of the community.

Chapter 3: What a Dialogue is *Not*

Not every conversation rises to the level of dialogue we've been talking about.[6] One way to make progress on a subject is to say what it is **not**. A dialogue is **not** simply an exchange of ideas, compromise, leaderless conversations, or all talk and no action.

Dialogue is not simply an exchange of ideas

Some people think that a dialogue is a simple exchange of ideas, where I talk and you nod your head, and then you talk and I nod my head. The end.

Certainly, one of the goals of a fruitful dialogue is the gathering of information. If I don't know why you don't want to follow a certain policy, or you think we should change a set system in the company, knowing why is vital.

But if dialogue is only an exchange of preferences, how does this really help when dealing with generational differences at work? I might *now* know the 'why' behind my colleague's behavior, but then what comes next?

Luckily, there is more to dialogue than an exchange of ideas. When there are differences or disagreements at work, external and industry standards can be used and applied to help steer the conversation partners towards the best answer.

Dialogue is not the same as compromise

When two people who have different ideas come together to hold a dialogue, what is the goal? Is it that both parties will get half of what they originally wanted?

This is not the goal of dialogue. The process of being in dialogue changes us, in that we are actively communicating, in real time, with our colleagues in order to listen to their concerns and perspectives, and to be listened to in kind. Through this process of collaboration, we make way for the Third Way to emerge. The Third Way takes place when we work together, not against each other.

The Third Way is best seen in the everyday conversations where a shift takes place in us, and our colleagues, simply by being in proximity, (Zoom counts).[7] Through the power of communication, who knows what's going to take place? I might slightly shift or change entirely, or you, the org, or the leader might change.

Dialogue takes us out of fighting for our rigid and limited positions and shows us what the positions are rooted in. It is in this discovery that creativity, engagement, and understanding takes place. Dialogue frees us from the limited vision that compromise is the best available option when people disagree.

Dialogue is not leaderless conversations

By in large, work environments are not democratic, where everyone's 'vote' or preference counts equally. While there are a variety of legitimate power structures that can be utilized in a company to bring about the good of the employees and those they serve, someone, or a team or board, makes the final decisions and, therefore, has the deciding vote.

What this means for dialogues at work is that the goal of these conversations is not to collect preferences and enact what the majority wants. Rather, the point is to understand our colleagues, ourselves, and set and reset expectations.

Imagine you have three colleagues where two are in their 20s and one is in their early 60s. The coworkers in their 20s dislike the company policy of 'no holes in jeans at work' and disregard the policy. The older employee is frustrated by her colleagues disregarding the dress code.

Through a conversation they come to understand each other's point of view. Now what?

While there are a variety of different options of what to do next, who decides on whether to change the dress code, enforce the current dress code, or keep it as is and turn a blind eye to dress code violations?

The mere fact of their dialogue does not mean they get to decide and change company policy. This is the leadership's responsibility.

But a good leader models and encourages dialogue and input. A good leader isn't simply acting out of personal preference (when these preferences impact others), but according to what is reasonable for the company and its people.

In this example of dress code issues, those in charge of making these decisions should take seriously the voices of the employees impacted and what the standard practices are in their given industry.

Through the practice of dialogue, something as simple but important as evaluating the dress code comes about in an organic and fruitful way.

This is an opportunity to reset expectations as to what is appropriate to wear in the organization, and why.

Dialogue is not all talk and no action

You may be concerned that if we are in constant dialogue with colleagues, nothing will ever get done!

Quite the contrary.

If you are in regular and fruitful dialogue with colleagues, everyone is freed up to work much more effectively and efficiently.

Why? Because time is spent on the front end of a project setting clear expectations, leaving room for questions, creativity, and clarity, which all increase buy-in. Time is not as likely to be wasted because lines of communication are open, freeing people to ask questions when needed.

Another reason dialogue leads to higher productivity is because time is not sucked into the black and poisonous hole of gossip.

If you want an engaged and high performing team, model and promote dialogue.

Chapter 4: When *We Decide Not* to invest in *Dialogue*, what are the alternatives?

Let's suppose you don't want to engage in real dialogue. You think it's too much work, takes too much time, or won't make a difference.

If you don't engage in real dialogue, what are you opting for instead?

- Lack of understanding
- Lack of introspection
- Monologue
- Silence
- Not listening
- Not being heard
- Arguing
- Stagnation
- Lack of community
- Reduced innovation
- Reduced revenue
- The impossibility of psychological safety

If you don't engage in real dialogue, you're choosing not to understand others.

How am I going to work with people I don't understand? If I am working based off a set of assumptions about professionalism, and you have a different set of assumptions, what is likely to occur?

I come to understand what motivates my colleagues, their standards about professionalism, and what the organization's unwritten rules of etiquette are through the process of the dialogue. I come to understand not only their 'what' but also their 'why.'

When we articulate our assumptions, and so do our colleagues, only then are we able to discuss and move forward with setting appropriate standards for the present team. These standards are set for and by the team, informed by reason, industry standards, and organizational needs.

Take the generational difference of adding either one or two spaces after a period and before starting a new sentence. Is it one or two spaces? This typographical issue may be irrelevant in your line of work. But in some workplaces, lines were and still are drawn and battles fought over the proper format.

These space battles were and are unnecessary. Holding regular conversations about changes in culture and the 'why' behind the changes assists the organization/team to stay current and leave no team member behind.

What is likely to happen when we don't take intentional time and effort to understand those we work with?

If you don't engage in real dialogue, you're choosing not to be introspective.

In this so-called modern generation war, lack of introspection runs rampant. The unreflective sentiments people hold about other generations is quite stunning.

If I am not in dialogue with my colleagues, I am much more likely to tell myself stories about other people's behavior, where they are the villain and I am the saint. They've caused me pain through their lack of professional and basic common decency, and I'm just here, doing my job!

There is a kind of luxury of living in the imaginary world where coworkers and bosses are the offenders, and we are the innocent. Yet, that's rarely the case. *Let me be clear – I'm talking about the everyday, run of the mill issues that happen at work, not crimes.*[8]

Normalizing dialogue and holding difficult conversations requires us to take stock of our actions. What is my role in this situation? What specifically is the issue, as I see it? What could I have done differently, or could I change moving forward?

When we opt to have conversations, real dialogues, we start to see and take responsibility for our part in the current situation.

What do you think is the likely outcome when we forgo dialogue with colleagues from other generations, and with it, the necessary introspection it entails?

If you don't engage in real dialogue, you're choosing monologue.

A monologue is one person talking. They are on the stage, and you are the audience. It's a one-way form of communication.

If you are not in conversation with those around you, you're just talking at them or being talked at.

Talking at someone is appropriate under certain circumstances. Sometimes we need to give and receive information. We simply need the facts or plan of action. The problem comes when this is the primary and default mode of communication. When this happens, the casualties are both communication and our engagement.

The problem with monologuing is not the form, but when it's used. Talking at colleagues, treating them as simple listeners and not partners, can leave the person talked at feeling unseen, uncared for, and with a bad taste in their mouth about the person doing the monologuing. The person monologuing can be seen as self-obsessed, or at least as not caring about the colleague they just talked at.

During your office interactions ask yourself, "Is this a real back and forth conversation, or could my audience be substituted for a brick wall?"

When someone doesn't care who they are talking at, we tend to minimize what they are saying. When we feel disposable or interchangeable, that the speaker doesn't care who they are talking at, the impact of their words is discounted or dismissed, and we take it less seriously. If they aren't respecting me, why should I care about what they are saying?

How do you feel when others talk at you?

If you train people to be quiet and just listen, then the real questions, concerns, and ideas they have fall further away from you. You won't get the vital pieces of information to make the best decisions, and you won't get others to partner with you in a way that encourages them to bring their 'A' game.

If you are only told what to do and never consulted about workplace norms, what is the likely outcome?

If you don't engage in real dialogue, you're choosing silence.

There is a time for silence.

There is a time for listening, reflecting, and doing the work. But, if all you have is silence, this is a sign people are checked out in a significant way.

Silence can be deafening. Consider what it feels like to be working in a place where the outdated adage, usually reserved for children, 'You should be seen and not heard,' is your reality. Does this lead to a healthy work environment?[9] If you hear nothing from your colleagues, ask yourself:

- Why is there only silence?
- What is being unsaid?
- What am I not hearing?
- What opportunities are being lost to the silence?
- What connections and collaborations are not being made?

If your team or organization turns a blind eye to generational wants, needs, and experiences of colleagues, what is the likely outcome?

If you don't engage in real dialogue, you're choosing not to listen to people.

Let me give you a recipe for a dying work culture: not listening to those around you. When we don't exercise the dialogue muscle about everyday issues, fruitful dialogue addressing serious issues is unlikely.

How are we going to find out about emerging problems and possibilities? How are we going to find out what is and what isn't working?

When leaders don't listen to the people they lead, what do you think is likely to happen?

Consider your own experiences. When you were listened to by the leaders and bosses you've had, what did that inspire in you?

Not only do we need managers and leaders to listen to their reports, but we also need employees to listen to those to whom they report. A lack of listening and paying attention is usually a sign of disrespect or despair. When the people on your team aren't listening to leadership, how can we expect to have a functioning and well-ordered workplace?

If you choose not to listen to what coworkers of different generations want, need and experience, what is the likely outcome?

If you don't engage in real dialogue, you're choosing not to be heard.

Have you ever taken a company survey, where they state they want to know about your experiences? What happens next in most cases?

The people who fill out the survey never know.

If a change is made, it is rarely seen by those who noted the issue on the survey. This results in increased disillusionment when we are asked what we think and in response we get a big black void staring back at us.

When people feel there is no one listening to them, the mantra pops up 'they don't care about me.' As soon as people feel like they are not cared for, they are likely to stop caring about their work.

It's a waste to miss out on what your people see. At all levels, employees gain insights about what does and doesn't work, what might be more efficient, what's impeding their productivity, etc. How will you know what's really going on if you don't have a working mechanism for finding out?

If there are not clear and consistent ways for employees from all generations to feel heard, what is the likely outcome?

If you don't engage in real dialogue, you're choosing to argue.

My childhood best friend lived directly across the street from me. For years we played together, having loads of fun. I distinctly remember having an argument with her, I don't remember about what, but we were standing at the edge of our respective driveways yelling at each other.

This is the picture I have in my head when I think about arguing: two children wearing themselves out shouting across the street at each other. No listening involved, no care or understanding for the other. Just me vs. you, the one with the hottest air winning.

At work, arguing is unprofessional and takes you away from the goal of understanding, engagement, buy-in, and treating coworkers with care.

We are certain to have many disagreements at work. The art is in disagreeing well through dialogue instead of reverting to childish arguing.

If arguing is the substitute for adult-to-adult dialogue at work, what is the likely outcome?

If you don't engage in real dialogue, you're choosing stagnation.

Creating an environment where innovation and creativity in the workplace emerge means dialogue is enabled and expected. When we don't have dialogue about what went well, what didn't, how to make something better, and whether to change directions entirely or stay the course, we get stuck in the past.

Change management is the name of the game. When you and your organization resist productive change, the result is bad for business and the people who work there. Change, in the right way, at the right time, for the right reasons, is a reality we must embrace.

When it comes to having a healthy work environment, where your colleagues come from multiple generations, if you opt out of dialogue and maintain the status quo, what is likely to happen?

If you don't engage in real dialogue, you're choosing a lack of community.

People are lonely at work.[10] You may say, "So what? Work is not for building your personal-friend empire. It's for work. Do it and leave. Find community elsewhere."

By nature, we are social creatures.[11] My social media is filled with people hating on their work colleagues, barely containing their anger until their virtual meeting is over, or they are in their cars, screaming and ranting.

I hear, repeatedly, how they are not there to make friends; they are there simply to work. No matter what the company says, we are not 'family.'

As to the 'family' part of this sentiment, I absolutely agree. Work is not your family. Your boss isn't your mother/father. Your work can fire/lay you off tomorrow.

While work is not your family, there are meaningful and important relationships we can develop to make work not only a humane place to be, but a place where we can experience joy and belonging.[12]

Show me a workplace that has brittle or hostile relationships among colleagues that is thriving. **You can't**. This is not how people work.

Since we need proper and professional levels of community at work to work excellently, what is likely to happen in an organization that doesn't make space for real dialogue among the generations?

If you don't engage in real dialogue, you're choosing to reduce innovation.

Innovation can come from anyone, of any age. Innovation is likely to take place where colleagues of different backgrounds and experiences value each other's insights and contributions.[13]

Where there is basic distrust of colleagues' abilities based simply on age, lack of innovation is going to be one of the many casualties an organization faces.

Consider the conditions that encourage innovation in you. On the other hand, what stifles your creativity and innovation? Do you know how your current colleagues would answer these questions?

A great way to find out is to ask! This is a low-stakes way to start a habit of dialogue with colleagues. I encourage you to put this book down, find a colleague if you're at work (and if not, then someone around you), and ask them, "Under what conditions are you the most creative and innovative? What conditions make it hard for you to be creative?"

Where there is a lack of dialogue between colleagues, how likely is innovation?

If you don't engage in real dialogue, you're choosing to reduce revenue.

Businesses want to appeal to the widest demographic possible to increase their pool of potential clients and workforce.

Where there is hostility, dismissiveness, and/or lack of communication between colleagues due to age differences, the bottom line of the organization will suffer for reasons enumerated above.

Businesses need to make money to keep the doors open. Not finding a way to engage your workforce due to differences in age is akin to burning money.

Do you want to waste money, lose opportunities, and fall behind in the marketplace? Since I know the answer is a resounding **no**, then you **must** find a way to move beyond the unnecessary and detrimental mentality of the generation wars and turn your multi-generational workforce into what they really are: golden opportunities not to be squandered.

This principle is not reserved for the business owner. As a professional, you will be more successful and likely earn more money if you know how to work well with all kinds of people.

If you don't engage in real dialogue, you're choosing to make psychological safety impossible.

Psychological safety is the belief an employee has that they can speak up without fear of retribution.

If people are vilified or minimized due to their age, they won't speak up, which means they won't be as engaged. They will demonstrate less buy-in and loyalty, and your workplace culture will be trending towards toxicity.

In an environment where high-level dialogue is habitually practiced, a by-product likely to emerge is psychological safety.

Under the conditions of the generation war, you can't achieve psychological safety. People will not be empowered to create, say what isn't working, or tell the truth as they see it.

If you are not actively working to create and maintain psychological safety at work, what is the likely outcome?

Chapter 5: What a Dialogue Requires of Us

Real dialogue makes demands on us.

Dialogue is an activity. It isn't passive. It requires we show up and participate. It requires more than our mere presence.

A dialogue requires:

- Self-awareness
- Curiosity
- A willingness and genuine interest in listening
- Excellent listening skills
- A desire to collaborate

Dialogue gives us the opportunity to:

- Be engaged in our environment
- Model professionalism
- Set civility standards

Dialogue requires self-awareness

It is important to know where you stand and why. How certain are you about your conclusions? What evidence do you have? Have you ever been mistaken or misguided in the past?

If you lack self-awareness, how can you entertain that there may be a different path to take or other legitimate perspectives? To be a good conversation partner, we must carefully consider and be able to articulate our positions, and the reasons motivating our positions.

Imagine Sue. She is making you mad because of her work ethic. Being self-aware requires you, for example, to be aware of your work standards, how you got them, why you value them, whether or not they're outdated, how you measure up to the standards you set for others, whether your standards meet, exceed, or fall short of the standards in your current organization.

Within this self-awareness, there needs to be enough humility and flexibility to recognize that some of your thoughts and ideas may need to be amended. You and I are fallible. We make mistakes, and entering a real dialogue gives us the opportunity to hold, on the one hand, our robust set of beliefs, and on the other hand, remain open to the possibility of change given a new set of information.

Dialogue requires curiosity

Self-awareness leads to curiosity. Just as dialogue requires that we are curious about ourselves and our positions, it's just as important to be curious about those we are in conversation with. What do they know that we might not? What does this colleague see that I do not? Does this colleague have a different goal in mind? What piece of information might they lack that has led them to their conclusion?

Back to Sue. Instead of stewing about her work ethic or lack thereof, ask yourself questions about her, such as:

- What does Sue think about her behavior?
- Why might she be behaving this way?
- What was her onboarding process?
- What is happening within the organization so that she thinks her behavior is appropriate?
- What is Sue getting right?
- Why am I bothered by her behavior?

Deciding to pause and get curious about colleagues' work habits and behaviors instead of rushing to judgement encourages dialogue and lessens the unnecessary gulf that can arise due to generational differences.

Dialogue requires a willingness and genuine interest in listening

If you think a colleague has nothing to offer you or your organization, you are unlikely to enter a good-faith dialogue. It's simple. You can't fake being a good conversation partner. If I see you tapping your foot, just waiting for me to finish speaking so you can start talking about your views, I won't see you as someone who is interested and invested in the process of the dialogue.

You might say, "Well, that's true. I don't really care what they have to say. And besides, I already know what they're going to say. No need to go through the motions of pretending to listen."

If this is your attitude, you are right. You are not ready to have a conversation. I know I don't want to have conversations with those who feel this way about what matters to me, and I bet you feel the same way.

So, what are we to do if we genuinely think we already know what they're going to say?

Let me tell you the truth – you're missing the point.

The act of listening requires we treat people as people and not as objects. Something magical happens between people when they listen and are heard. It is in this human-to-human interaction, when people are treated with respect, that progress is made.

This progress is about solving issues, hearing and understanding new pieces of information, and building stronger working relationships.

Dialogue requires excellent listening skills

For this interaction to occur, we need to know how to listen. We need to know how to be present, what to do with our bodies, how to understand our emotions and reactions, and how to move through sometimes complicated information.

Consider Tina. Tina is 24. You are 67 and so is your friend Mitch. She wants to talk to you about Mitch.

Mitch is her new client and happens to be your longtime friend.

Tina asks to privately meet with you in the conference room. As soon as Tina brings up your friend, Mitch, you tense up. You just know she's going to start trash talking him. *Besides, Mitch is a new client. Why is she running him down? Certainly, Tina must know Mitch is one of my best friends!*

In reality, Tina wants to talk with you to figure out the best way to communicate with Mitch. She also wants to talk about the fact that she's increasingly feeling uncomfortable around him.

You have a choice to make. You can pause, take a breath, begin to de-escalate yourself, relax your body and be present to listen to what Tina has to say, or not.

If you choose to be mentally and physically present, listening for what the issue or issues are, you will find out what's going on, possibly assisting your colleague, your friend, and your company. If you choose to react and get upset because you think Tina is about to slander your friend, what are you going to get? For one, you are sending a message to Tina that you are volatile, not interested in hearing her out or helping her, now or in the future.

We act on the information we have. The more we make ourselves available to listen excellently, the more information we have, which leads to better overall decisions and outcomes.

Many of the generational issues people have at work are due to an underdeveloped desire and ability to listen well.

Dialogue requires a desire to collaborate

If you are a lone wolf at work or think your colleagues have nothing to offer, you are **not** a candidate for genuine dialogue.[14] If, however, you think your colleague or colleagues just might have something valuable to offer, then proceed.

The very nature of dialogue is collaborative. I start with my position, and you with yours. As we move through the process of the dialectic, we gather new information and therefore are changed in some way. A new understanding emerges, even if an agreed solution is not immediately reached.

This exchange of ideas and creativity is not about compromise. Through the collaborative process of a real dialogue, something new emerges.

This is exciting and wonderful news! Innovation, creativity, change, becoming unstuck, and so much more are the byproducts of the collaborative nature of dialogue.

Another valuable fruit of dialogue is the trust it can produce between the people collaborating. When I invest in a collaborative dialogue with you, and we move through the hard parts, I see you as someone who is willing to work diligently, do tough things, listen to me, and contribute. This raises your social capital in my eyes because I've experienced what it's like to work through something difficult, and I've experienced how you acted, how you treated me, and the product of our dialogue.

When we aren't in dialogue with people who differ from us generationally, it's easier to 'other' them. The more distance I create between me and you, and the more I minimize you, the less likely I am to have the desire to collaborate.

Dialogue gives us the opportunity to model professionalism

Yelling, subverting, talking over, squashing dissent, silencing other voices, and not caring about your colleagues are signs of selfishness, lack of emotional intelligence, and unprofessionalism. The person who can't hold a genuine dialogue is untrustworthy.

The professional is on the lookout for new information, greater insights, and treating people excellently. Giving the gift of dialogue with another person expresses to that person, as well as to the others in the office watching, that you genuinely are interested in treating people with respect and want them to thrive.

A true professional is interested in seeing people as people first, and as business associates somewhere down the line.

Therefore, being a professional is about working with people who are from different generations. Modeling professionalism in this case shows others that it is unwise to bow to agism and age-based stereotypes.

Dialogue gives us the opportunity to set civility standards

For an office environment to thrive, there must be reasonable, known, *and* enforced civility standards. What are the rules of engagement here? What kind of behavior ought we expect from our colleagues and ourselves?

There should be hard conversations at work. There should be differences of opinion when it comes to the use of resources, direction of the organization, developing and executing plans, etc. Dialogue encourages colleagues to be able to talk about difficult topics in a controlled environment. This is the art of disagreeing well.

One of the first casualties when we don't engage in real dialogue with those of different generations is civility. When basic standards of civility are not set and adhered to in an organization and/or team, you will see:

- Colleagues undermining each other
- Factions
- Gossip
- Inability to work well and collaborate
- Lack of retention

- Low engagement, creativity, and innovation

Civility standards ought to be set by the group to whom they apply. This means a continued open dialogue to set, evaluate, reassess, and refine civility standards to keep them current and relevant.[15]

How do we set and get buy-in of employee-centric civility standards? You guessed it ... genuine dialogue.

Dialogue gives us the opportunity to engage in our work environment

Engagement is vital to have a high performing work environment. If we feel at odds with colleagues because of an age barrier we don't know how to address, how are we to be fully engaged when we start to view others as obstacles to put up with or get around?

What are signs of engagement at work?

- Collaboration
- Collegiality
- Creativity and innovation
- High attendance and retention rates
- High productivity
- Lack of gossip
- Stellar customer service

Since it's a given every organization wants employees to be high performers, age gaps and agism must be addressed to free people to be engaged. To do this, we must be able to hold fruitful dialogues with our colleagues.

Chapter 6: When to Have Dialogue, and When to Hold Back

When to Engage in Dialogue at Work

When situations become difficult or tense, for many people the default response is to refrain from dialogue.[16] Instead of holding a difficult conversation, people tend to figure it out alone or gossip. This narrative of going at it alone or gossiping needs to be disrupted and replaced with a new default: when in doubt, talk it out.

Why should you engage in dialogue at work? Here are a few good reasons:

- If you don't want to burn money and waste time
- If you need to build connections
- If you want innovation
- If you want to build and maintain resilient and relevant teams and organizations
- If you want to create ongoing psychological safety, where people feel they can speak up without fear of retribution
- If you want to develop consensus and/or buy-in
- If you want to know about potential barriers or opportunities

Dialogue should take place both one-on-one and within the group. It should be regular, just as we need to regularly set, re-set, and assess our expectations.

The more you make it a habit to engage in real dialogue as a matter of standard practice, the less likely you are to fall-prey to gossip and unhelpful narratives about colleagues from other generations.

Dialogue should be a habitual practice and the default go-to as soon as issues arise. The longer you wait, the trickier real dialogues become.

When *Not* to Engage in Dialogue at Work

While we ought to seek to engage in good-faith discussions with our coworkers, there are times when dialogue is the wrong way to go.

- **If you feel unsafe** with your colleague, physically or psychologically, don't engage. Seek assistance from a coworker, boss, or a third party.
- If you are feeling unable to hold a respectful conversation, don't engage at that time. De-escalate yourself until you are composed and ready to treat the other person well.

Sometimes our emotions run high and the particular narrative we've told ourselves about the colleague in question has us assessing the situation incorrectly. Having assistance from an outside party can help us cool down and reassess the situation, freeing us to hold a fruitful and professional conversation.

Sometimes, the other person misbehaves, and we ought not put ourselves in a situation to be abused.

Ongoing dialogue is necessary in establishing and maintaining healthy work environments. However, there are a few who will try to use dialogue as a club and tool of manipulation.

I want to make this abundantly clear: **No One Should Be Mistreated at Work**. While we owe everyone a high level of civility and basic human respect, we must also treat ourselves in kind. We owe it to ourselves to insist on being treated respectfully at work.

Important Neon-Flashing Note

Since we, as a culture, have gotten out of the habit of knowing how to talk with people we disagree with, it can feel as if someone is bullying us just because they disagree with our position, values, or facts.

Disagreement is not synonymous with misbehaving. Real dialogue is the act and art of disagreeing well.

The way to move forward and rewrite this feeling and narrative that disagreement equals disrespect is through the habitual and ritualized[17] act of civilly and respectfully discussing issues people disagree about. No name calling. No 'othering.' Even the most practiced practitioner of high-level dialogue can feel psychologically unsettled in a conversation when they experience pushbacks from the other side.

Thus, we ought not equate difficulty with misbehaving[18] and civility violations.

Chapter 7: Creating a Dialogue Mindset

When considering holding a difficult conversation with a colleague, a major appeal for doing it is that once you've had the talk it's over and you can move forward.

While it's true that a dialogue is an event occurring at a specific time and place, developing and nurturing a dialogue mindset is vital.

The best way to ensure good working relationships is to be able to talk about whatever needs to be discussed, from the small and easy issues all the way to the difficult, tricky, and messy problems.

If we think about dialogues as isolated events we just need to get through, we miss out on what really needs to happen: a conversion and reorientation towards expecting dialogue to be a regular feature of office life.

Instead of seeing dialogue as one offs, a dialogue mindset shifts you into a way of being, thinking, and acting, setting the expectation of talking, articulating, and finding the best path forward and away from mindreading, silos, disengagement, and gossip.

Imagine what might change in you and your work environment if your expectation was to notice and talk about issues early, often, swiftly, and justly.

- **Early**, before they snowball
- **Often**, not waiting for the annual review or some far-off appointed time to discuss issues

- **Swiftly**, instead of engaging in an unnecessary drawn-out bloated process, where people are dragging their feet
- **Justly,** where everyone is treated with care and respect

Having a dialogue mindset is a must for the engaged worker.

Imagine what it would be like to work in a place that doesn't value your perspective, knowledge, or experience? What would it be like to work in a place where the message is, 'Keep your head down, don't ask questions, and do as we tell you.'

That is an inhumane place. That is a place that will not attract or retain talent. That work environment is set up for misery and burns money on the pyre of their own failure to treat workers with dignity, respect, and as incredibly valuable to making the business a success.

The choice is yours. What kind of professional do you want to be?

Section II: A Very Brief Look at the World of Work in the U.S. for the Past 60 Years

Chapter 8: The Way Change and Innovation Work

You consider something a technology if it deviates from what you're currently experiencing. With a rare exception, no one reading this book will consider electric lights in their home a technology. It is normal for you. You grew up with it. In fact, when you experience a loss of electricity, such as sometimes happens during a storm, it feels unnatural. You wait for the electricity to be restored and with it a sense of normalcy.

Of course, indoor electricity is a technology, an advancement. But it doesn't have the *feeling* of something new because it is our normal. We don't have to adopt our habits and habitats to accommodate it, because indoor electricity is completely embedded and enmeshed in our everyday life. We don't think about electricity until the unusual happens and we are without electricity.

To understand and work well with our colleagues from different generations, it is helpful to see from their perspective what is considered normal and a standard for them, and what is *new* technology.

Normal: what we grow up with.

New technology: what comes along and is adopted sometime in our teens.

With this in mind, let's consider what has transpired in the last 60 years of work, leading us to today. We will look at what the norms were in a large organization from the perspective of a 20-something year old entering the world of work in corporate America in different areas.[19] This will give us a glimpse of what they considered normal, the baseline, as they entered the world of work.[20]

This section was generated through a conversation between myself and ChatGPT beginning in December of 2024, with modifications made by me.

Chapter 9: Let's go to Work in the U.S. in 1965[21]

22

Imagine you are 20 years old in 1965 and starting your career in corporate America. The nation is optimistic yet rigidly structured, influenced by the post-WWII industrial boom. The workplace reflects a culture of conformity, professionalism, and hierarchy.

Basic Office Policies

Corporate environments were highly structured. Employees adhered to strict rules regarding behavior and productivity, with little room for deviation.

Professionalism was emphasized, and consistency was valued over creativity or innovation at lower levels.

Dress Code Norms

Men wore dark suits, white shirts and ties, while women wore modest skirts, dresses, or tailored suits with low heels. Personal expression in attire was uncommon because the emphasis was on uniformity and professionalism.

Working Hours

The standard workday was 9-to-5, Monday through Friday. Overtime was common but rarely compensated for salaried employees. Arriving on time and being present during work hours was critical to maintaining a good reputation.

Basic Expectations

Employees were expected to show loyalty, respect authority, and focus on their assigned tasks. Questioning authority or suggesting alternative methods were rare, and success was largely defined by compliance and perseverance.

Leadership Styles

Leadership was authoritarian and hierarchical. Managers directed and employees followed, with decisions rarely open to challenge. Innovation and collaboration were not encouraged among lower-level employees.

Communication Methods

Face-to-face meetings, memos, and handwritten notes were the primary methods of communication. Telephones were used internally, but long-distance calls were expensive and used sparingly. Typewritten documents were central to communication and record-keeping.

Technology and Tools

- **Manual Typewriter**: Essential for creating documents.

- **Paperwork**: Stacks of paper and memos were always present.

- **Rolodex**: A staple for organizing business contacts.

- **Rotary Telephone**: The primary communication tool.

Computers existed but were limited to specialized rooms and used by highly trained operators.

Work-Life Balance Practices

Work-life balance was not a focus. Employees often prioritized their jobs over their personal lives, and vacation days were rarely encouraged. Ambition was measured by dedication to the company.

Career Progression Expectations

Loyalty was the cornerstone of career advancement. Employees often stayed with the same company for decades, with promotions based on tenure rather than merit or innovation.

Attitudes toward Diversity and Inclusion

Corporate America was largely homogenous, with white men dominating leadership positions. Women and minorities were confined to lower-level or administrative roles. The Civil Rights Movement was beginning to challenge these norms, but workplace change was slow.

Social and Recreational Workplace Culture

Social events such as company picnics and holiday parties were formal and hierarchical. Watercooler talk and informal camaraderie were limited by productivity expectations. Smoking in the office was common, with ashtrays often on desks.

Chapter 10: Let's go to Work in the U.S. in 1975

23

Imagine you are 20 years old in 1975, entering the workforce during a time of societal change and shifting norms. The Vietnam War is ending, Watergate has shaken confidence in authority, and cultural movements are influencing corporate America. While the workplace remains formal, cracks in rigid conformity are beginning to show.

Basic Office Policies

Policies emphasized professionalism, but there was a growing awareness of employee satisfaction. Work environments started to balance structure with an emerging need for flexibility. Loyalty to the company was still expected, but some individual freedoms were beginning to be acknowledged.

Dress Code Norms

Men wore suits but began experimenting with more color and patterns. Wide ties and bold designs reflected the shifting culture. Women increasingly wore pantsuits alongside traditional skirts and dresses.

Working Hours

The standard 9-to-5 schedule persisted, though overtime remained common when deadlines loomed. Flextime was introduced experimentally, hinting at future changes. Employees were still judged by their physical presence in the office.

Basic Expectations

While productivity and loyalty were still paramount, the counterculture movement subtly influenced workplace dynamics. Employees began to feel more comfortable questioning authority and seeking fulfillment beyond their roles. Creativity and independent thinking were increasingly valued, though not yet widespread.

Leadership Styles

Leadership remained hierarchical but softened slightly. Managers began incorporating motivational strategies and sought input from employees more often. Collaboration was limited but growing as a concept.

Communication Methods

Face-to-face communication and memos were still the norm, but telephones were used more frequently for interoffice communication. Computers were rare but becoming more accessible, mainly for specialized departments. Electric typewriters became the standard tool for office work.

Technology and Tools

- **Calculator**: Desktop calculators were a must for financial and data tasks.

- **Electric Typewriter**: Faster and quieter than manual models.

- **Paperwork**: Still dominated the office environment.

- **Rolodex**: Remained essential for managing contacts.

- **Rotary Telephone**: Still widely used for communication.

Computers were still limited to specialized rooms and used by trained operators (the Apple 1 didn't appeared until 1976.)

Work-Life Balance Practices

Dual-income households were becoming more common, leading to increased awareness of work-life balance. Companies introduced limited employee assistance programs, though these were in their infancy.

Career Progression Expectations

Career advancement was still largely tenure-based, though innovation and results were beginning to play a role. Younger employees started to explore mobility as a viable career strategy, challenging the idea of staying at one company for life.

Attitudes toward Diversity and Inclusion

The Civil Rights Movement and second-wave feminism spurred incremental changes. More women and minorities were entering the workforce, but they remained underrepresented in leadership roles. Equal opportunity initiatives were just starting to take hold.

Social and Recreational Workplace Culture

Social activities became more casual. Office parties, recreational clubs, and after-work gatherings gained traction. These events promoted camaraderie, though hierarchies still influenced interactions.

Chapter 11: Let's go to Work in the U.S. in 1985

24

Imagine you are 20 years old in 1985 and starting your career in a world influenced by the Cold War, the rise of the personal computer, and a booming economy. The workplace was evolving rapidly, with a focus on innovation, efficiency, and competition.

Basic Office Policies

Efficiency and results became focal points of office policies. Employees were encouraged to learn and adapt to technological advancements. Professionalism and structure still prevailed. Policies reflected the era's growing competitive nature.

Dress Code Norms

Professional attire remained standard, but power dressing emerged. Men wore sharp suits, while women embraced power suits with shoulder pads, symbolizing assertiveness and ambition. Business attire reflected the more competitive ethos of the time.

Working Hours

The 9-to-5 schedule remained typical, but overtime increased as 'workaholism' became a badge of honor. Employees were expected to work late or on weekends to climb the corporate ladder.

Basic Expectations

Adaptability and technical proficiency became critical, as computers and automation entered offices. Employees were expected to embrace innovation, meet high productivity standards, and contribute to the company's goals.

Leadership Styles

Leadership began incorporating motivational strategies, though it remained hierarchical. Managers encouraged productivity and innovation while experimenting with collaborative approaches and team-building exercises.

Communication Methods

Phone calls and memos were still common, but email emerged as a game-changer for communication in early adopting companies. Fax machines became integral for document sharing. Computers began streamlining communication processes.

Technology and Tools

- **CRT Monitor**: Dominated desk setups.

- **Electric Typewriter**: Still used in some offices but declining in favor of computers.

- **Fax Machine**: Revolutionized document sharing.

- **Personal Computer**: A growing staple for word processing and data tasks.

- **Rolodex**: Still present but beginning to be supplemented by digital tools.

Work-Life Balance Practices

Work-life balance was deprioritized as the competitive corporate culture encouraged employees to sacrifice personal time for career success. The expectation of being 'always available' began to take root.

Career Progression Expectations

Merit-based promotions gained importance, though tenure and loyalty still played significant roles. Employees with technical skills and innovative ideas had an edge in career advancement.

Attitudes toward Diversity and Inclusion

Affirmative action policies and increased societal awareness brought diversity to the forefront. Women and minorities gained more visibility in the workplace, though leadership roles were still dominated by white men.

Social and Recreational Workplace Culture

Networking and team building became essential. Casual happy hours, holiday parties, and recreational clubs reflected a more relaxed social atmosphere compared to previous decades.

Chapter 12: Let's go to Work in the U.S. in 1995

Imagine you are 20 years old in 1995 and entering a workplace shaped by globalization, the early internet, and the tech boom. Corporate America was undergoing a digital transformation, with innovation driving significant changes in tools, communication, and culture, though many workplaces remained deeply hierarchical.

Basic Office Policies

Policies became more flexible and focused on adaptability. While professionalism and structure remained, collaboration and innovation were emphasized in theory, but rigid procedures and micromanagement often persisted.

Dress Code Norms

Business casual began to replace traditional formal attire in many workplaces. Men wore slacks and polo shirts or collared shirts without ties, while women moved toward slacks, blouses, and comfortable professional wear. Casual Fridays became a widespread practice.

Working Hours

The standard 9-to-5 schedule remained, but the availability of personal computers and email extended work beyond office hours. An 'always-on' culture took root without much institutional support for boundaries.

Basic Expectations

Employees were expected to be proficient with computers and adapt to rapidly changing technologies. Innovation and teamwork were praised, but many workplaces rewarded conformity and long hours over creativity.

Leadership Styles

Management books and seminars encouraged leadership styles to shift toward empowerment and collaboration, but traditional command-and-control management remained dominant in practice.

Communication Methods

Email became the dominant method of communication, supplementing phone calls and in-person meetings. Fax machines were still widely used, and internet communication began gaining traction.

Technology and Tools

- CRT Monitors and Early Internet
- Email
- Fax Machines and Printers
- Personal Computers
- Rolodex fading in importance

Work-Life Balance Practices

Flexibility began to emerge but remained rare. Long hours were often normalized, and work-life balance was discussed more than it was practiced.

Career Progression Expectations

Career paths were increasingly based on skills, but seniority and internal politics still heavily influenced advancement.

Attitudes toward Diversity and Inclusion

Diversity initiatives gained traction, but progress was slow. Most leadership teams remained largely homogeneous, and discrimination persisted beneath surface-level policies.

Social and Recreational Workplace Culture

Team-building exercises and after-work gatherings became popular, but often participation was seen as mandatory for career advancement.

Chapter 13: Let's go to Work in the U.S. in 2005

26

Imagine you are 20 years old in 2005 and starting your career during a time when the internet had become central to daily life, smartphones were emerging, and globalization was transforming corporate America.

Basic Office Policies

Corporate policies increasingly focused on results and flexibility. Ethical standards and corporate responsibility were emphasized publicly, but high-pressure environments and burnout remained widespread.

Dress Code Norms

Business casual was the standard, with a focus on professionalism and comfort.

Working Hours

Work schedules grew more flexible, and mobile technology kept employees tethered to work well beyond office hours. 'Flexible' often meant working more, but differently.

Basic Expectations

Tech-savviness was critical, and collaboration across time zones was expected. Yet micromanagement and rigid project oversight remained common.

Leadership Styles

Although management books promoted mentorship and empowerment, many managers maintained strict hierarchical control, and regular feedback was often used more for compliance than growth.

Communication Methods

Email and instant messaging became primary tools, with video conferencing emerging. Despite new tools, communication often remained top-down.

Technology and Tools

- Early Cloud-Based Tools
- Email and Instant Messaging
- Laptops
- Mobile Phones

Work-Life Balance Practices

Wellness initiatives appeared but were often superficial. Real cultural change around work-life balance lagged behind technological capabilities.

Career Progression Expectations

While individualized career paths were encouraged, loyalty to the organization still often mattered more than innovation in determining promotions.

Attitudes toward Diversity and Inclusion

Diversity and inclusion became institutionalized goals, but deep cultural change remained slow and often focused on optics rather than impact.

Social and Recreational Workplace Culture

Social activities blended in-person and online interactions. While virtual collaboration tools supported global teams, the reality of office life remained siloed and organizationally politically charged.

Chapter 14: Let's go to Work in the U.S. in 2015

27

Imagine you are 20 years old in 2015 and entering a workplace fully immersed in the digital age yet still carrying much of the old culture.

Basic Office Policies

Policies emphasized agility and innovation, but traditional bureaucratic structures often resisted true change.

Dress Code Norms

Casual attire became widely accepted, with employees often wearing jeans and sneakers. Professional attire was reserved for specific events or client interactions. Personal style was welcomed, reflecting a shift toward individuality.

Working Hours

Flexibility expanded, but the expectation to be available at all times remained, blurring the line between freedom and overwork.

Basic Expectations

Employees were expected to be lifelong learners, adapting to rapidly changing technologies. Collaboration, innovation, and problem-solving were critical skills. However, organizations still valued loyalty and internal politics over innovation in many cases.

Leadership Styles

Mentorship and empowerment were promoted, but hierarchical, command-driven leadership remained widespread, especially among middle management.

Communication Methods

Slack, video conferencing, and real-time tools became dominant, speeding up work expectations without reducing workload.

Technology and Tools

- Laptops
- Email
- AI-Driven Applications
- Cloud Computing
- Mobile-First Solutions

Work-Life Balance Practices

Wellness programs became more visible, but meaningful work-life boundaries often depended on individual managers rather than company culture.

Career Progression Expectations

Dynamic career paths expanded, but many still encountered slow advancements based on organizational politics rather than skills.

Attitudes toward Diversity and Inclusion

While diversity and inclusion became core corporate values, progress was uneven. Tokenism remained a serious problem in many industries.

Social and Recreational Workplace Culture

Global virtual collaborations and creative team events became common, but workplace engagement surveys showed persistent issues with disengagement and dissatisfaction.

Chapter 15: Let's go to Work in the U.S. in 2025

28

Imagine you are 20 years old in 2025 and entering a workplace reeling from the worldwide pandemic, theoretically designed around AI, sustainability, and purpose, though old habits still linger.

Basic Office Policies

Flexibility and innovation are emphasized, but many companies still struggle with micromanagement and outdated control structures.

Dress Code Norms

Dress codes are entirely task-specific, with most employees wearing casual, comfortable clothing. Productivity and creativity are prioritized over appearance.

Working Hours

Hybrid and asynchronous schedules are normal. However, since the worldwide pandemic of 2020, there is widespread disagreement about remote vs. in person work. Managing boundaries between work and life remains an individual responsibility rather than a cultural guarantee.

Basic Expectations

Change management, agile learning, and cross-functional collaboration are mandatory, but 'agility' sometimes masks poor planning and chaotic leadership.

Leadership Styles

Leadership is trending toward facilitation and psychological safety, but not all industries or companies have successfully made this cultural leap. Widespread disengagement and 'quiet quitting' are partially blamed on poor leadership.

Communication Methods

AI-enhanced tools, virtual reality spaces, and instant communication dominate. Face-to-face meetings are valued for building relationships.

Technology and Tools

- Laptops
- Advanced AI
- Quantum Computing
  Virtual Reality

Work-Life Balance Practices

Personal Time Off, PTO, and wellness resources are offered widely, but the actual usage depends on organizational trust and leadership follow-through.

Career Progression Expectations

Careers are dynamic and personalized, though job insecurity and the need for constant reskilling create new pressures.

Attitudes toward Diversity and Inclusion

Equity is embedded into many systems, but vigilance remains necessary to ensure AI systems don't replicate old biases. Instability as to the status of DEI initiatives are in flux due to the changing political climate.

Social and Recreational Workplace Culture

Global collaboration and purpose-driven initiatives are common, but burnout and disengagement still challenge even the most progressive companies.

Section III: What's the Problem? Causes of & Solutions to the Culture Wars at Work

Chapter 16: Technology

Oh, the promise of modern technology!

It will make our lives easier, give us more time, and make us rich! Who doesn't want that?

Technology has the power to unite us *and* sow discord and division.

The use of technology, or lack thereof, is fertile ground for generational battles with one side shouting to the other, "Convert your pdf yourself!" while the other side retorts, "Why don't you try making a phone call!"

Technology explodes the notion of the local, making the world flat. But with the new possibilities, overwhelm sets in all too often, stealing our time and attention as we consider using the new tech: which LLM, which presentation software, which social media platforms, should we use crypto currency?

Technology is constantly changing, and it's a time-suck. It takes time to learn the new, and it isn't always apparent if the new technology is:

1. Better than the old way,

2. Trivial, or

3. Vital.

If we are not careful, we can fall into the trap of relegating those who don't speak the newest tech language to the status of 'other' to be pitied, babied, or scorned because they have not adopted the 'new.'

We can also trick ourselves into trivializing and minimizing emerging technologies because we don't understand or 'like' them. This mentality can have the effect of rendering us unable to have an educated conversation about whether the new technology should be tested out, adopted, or skipped over.

When it comes to new and emerging technologies, consider the following questions when engaging in dialogue with your colleagues:

- What expectations are there to 'keep up?'
- Who's responsible for spotting the new technology, implementing the new, and training others?
- What pieces of technology do all workers need to know (vs. specialized knowledge)?
- What are we (this organization, this office, this team) going to do to ensure the proper use of technology, so that colleagues are not minimized due to their adoption, enthusiasm, or ill ease with technology?

Chapter 17: Work/Life Balance

What is work for, and how much of your lifetime should it require? What are reasonable working hours?[29]

There are shifting expectations as to what role work has in a life well lived. In the not-so-distant past, the picture of the good life was being a 'company man,' devoting the vast amount of a person's time, attention, and talents to the world of work.[30]

This often required working beyond the 9-5 into nights and weekends. The company, profession, and your role in it demanded to be the primary focus of life, claiming the priority of your time and attention.

The expectation of younger workers to 'pay their dues,' by sacrificing personal and family time for the job is strong, because that's what other generations experienced. Pay now, reward later.

Today, younger generations have a different take.[31] Many have witnessed the repugnant treatment of their parents/guardians in the workplace through firings, layoffs, and/or toxic work environments. They may have experienced a family member's entire profession being eliminated due to shifts in culture, technology, outsourcing, or poor management.

The lack of loyalty organizations demonstrated to the workforce has had a residual effect, leading to question why they should be loyal to their employer. This, among many other shifts in culture, have led to a real question, "How much does work deserve of my time, attention, and effort?"

This questioning of what is the appropriate work/life balance runs through the generations, with some asking the question in their first jobs, and others in their last. The world of work and culture has shifted greatly on this question of what role work should claim in our lives, with no clear answer emerging.

So, in the same workspace you have coworkers who have vastly different ideas of what it means to appropriately incorporate the *right* work/life balance.[32]

When it comes to expectations concerning work/life balance, consider the following questions when engaging in dialogue with your colleagues:

- What is working too much and what is working not enough?

- What is your work/life balance expectation? Why do you have this expectation? Where did it come from? Is this expectation serving you well?

- What is the work/life balance expectation where you work? How do people know this expectation? What is the written vs. unwritten expectation? Why is this the right balance?

Chapter 18: Loyalty

My father-in-law, from the silent generation, worked for Otis Elevator Company for over 40 years. It was his expectation when he entered the world of work to find a company and move up the ranks. He saw himself as loyal to his company.

How many people entering the work force today have the expectation or goal of working at one company until they retire? Not many.

What does it mean to be loyal to an organization? Is this a desirable or even reasonable quality to aspire to in the age of layoffs and shifting markets?

Loyalty is a two-way street: employers to employees, and employees to employers.

Loyalty of employers to employees is demonstrated by setting and maintaining healthy working conditions. This includes reasonable pay and benefits, good physical and psychological working conditions, and excellent leadership.

Disloyalty is seen in treating employees poorly through mismanagement, gaslighting, incivility, substandard pay, and lack of care.

Loyalty of employees toward employers is demonstrated through engagement and professionalism. Professionalism in the work you are doing, engagement with your team, and buy-in to the organizational mission.

The opposite of employee loyalty is a kind of sabotage, akin to dragging your company online or quiet quitting. Some see disloyalty as displaying selfishness, laziness, or unprofessionalism.

If this is the modern way to talk about loyalty, it's quite evident why loyalty is important to both employers and employees.[33]

The organizational benefits of having loyal employees are wide-ranging. Benefits include the institutional memories that excellent retained workers carry to saving the hefty price the organization is spared when they leave.[34]

When it comes to expectations concerning loyalty at work, consider the following questions when engaging in dialogue with your colleagues:

- What does loyalty mean to you? Is this a relevant value in today's world of work?
- What does loyalty mean to your colleagues and leadership?
- Should people be loyal to an organization, its mission, and/or your colleagues?
- What policies or lack thereof encourage people to be loyal?
- What policies or lack thereof encourage people to be disloyal?

- What practices and policies does the organization have in place that signal they are loyal to their employees?
- Which practices and policies send 'red flags' to employees that the organization does not care and is not/will not be loyal to them?
- What reasonable expectations of loyalty should be expected from both colleagues and the organization?

Chapter 19: Money

A few years ago, there was a fairly odd fixation on avocado toast in the U.S. Should young adults be eating it? Can they really afford it?

Summed up, the choices from the older generations appeared to be:

A. Either you have your avocado toast, coffee house coffee, drinks out about town, and, therefore, forever be a renter.

Or

B. Practice strict austerity measures by buying all your food and drink at the chain (not the fancy) grocery store, refrain from nights on the town, and, therefore, be able to afford to become a homeowner.

Given these choices, the typical response to the older generation was: hope you enjoy your home you bought for next to nothing, with your out-of-touch smug moral superiority!

What people value and choose to spend money on has much to do with the disdain generations have towards each other. A lack of respect for what each value.

<u>Why do the younger generations</u> think they deserve to have it all now? The big fancy cars, homes, and vacations. Instead, they should work (like I had to), squirrel it away, and wait until they've worked a few decades to feel the effects of the American Dream.

Why do the older generations think we will ever make enough to afford home ownership when we are swimming in student loan debt, the cost of rent is x% of our monthly income (unlike the y% you enjoyed when starting out). The American dream of a house with a white picket fence and all the trimmings is nothing more than a mirage. These promises of working hard and achieving financial stability feel like a lie.

When we buy into the culture-war narrative that our colleagues are out of touch about the cost of living, on either side of this equation, an unnecessary division can develop.

Can I trust 'them' with the budget when they have an unrealistic conception of what things cost and what is valuable?

Money suspicion has a way of creeping over into a general feeling of the 'other' as being unprofessional or untrustworthy to make the right decisions for the team or company.

When it comes to values and ideas surrounding money at work, consider the following questions when engaging in dialogue with your colleagues:

- Who is/who should be aware of the current pricing for the goods and services the organization uses, from color copies and ads, to materials for components, etc.?
- What expenditures do people on your team think are frivolous? What expenditures do

people on your team think are stingy or
ineffectual because not enough money is spent
on them?

- What should your group stop spending money
  on? What is the market evidence to support this
  claim?
- What should your group start spending money
  on? What is the market evidence to support this
  claim?
- What are the current best practices when it
  comes to what money should be spent on? Who
  is/should be involved in these decisions? What
  transparency is there/should there be for these
  conversations?

Chapter 20: Work Ethic

People don't want to work anymore! This frustration is an old tale.[35] The young people just don't want to work anymore, and once they are 'working,' their work ethic is awful!

What makes up this poor work ethic? The lamenter means one or more of the following:

- A lack of ambition
- A lack of motivation
- A lack of polish
- A lack of professionalism
- Entitlement to status, perks, or money
- Inexperience
- Not willing to stay with a project until the work is completed

And when younger generations scoff at the offerings of an organization and its work ethic expectations, could it be due to:

- A lack of leadership
- A lack of proper training
- A lack of transparency and communication
- Poor onboarding practices
- The leader or owner expects workers to care as much as they do about the success of the organization

- The organization's policies on compensation and/or promotion policies are stuck in a different time

When we hold onto the narrative that a colleague lacks the desire to work professionally or some of our colleagues have unreasonable and outdated conceptions of how much they ought to work, divisions take root.

Us vs. Them

This narrative about 'the other' can lead to self-fulfilling prophecies, since people tend to rise or fall to the expectations put on them.

Why talk to 'them,' since they don't care anyway?

If there is a difference in conceptions of proper work ethic in your organization, consider these questions:

- What is the proper work ethic here? What are the expectations? Why these expectations? Are these the proper expectations right now given the realities of work, the work force, and the ever-changing nature of work?
- Hold conversations about how retention, raises, and promotions work within the organization. What is valued and why? What are examples of work behaviors (work ethic) that resulted in promotions, being passed over, and being let go?

- Hold conversations about how to retain the best workers. The work ethic on the employee's side needs to be matched with appropriate loyalty on the employer's side.
- If the issue is a lack of experience, ask: what kind of proper opportunities for growth can we offer?
- If the issue is lack of perceived ambition: hold conversations to articulate for understanding company rewards and consequences of work behaviors. Ask employees what their goals are and what they'd like to achieve.
- If the issue is a lack of professional polish: hold conversations to articulate company standards about speech, attire, and similar professional standards.
- If the issue is a perceived sense of entitlement, set expectations for everyone on the team as to what the industry wide standards of work and rewards are.
- If the issue is not completing tasks in a timely manner, hold conversations about realistic working hours, comp time, and days off.
- If there is a perceived lack of motivation ask, what motivates you to do X?

Chapter 21: Cultural Shift

On my first international flight, I was in the 'non-smoking' section of the plane. About five rows behind me began the 'smoking' section. That smoking on planes is all but a relic of the past is to be celebrated, from my perspective. Some smokers may not see it this way.

Cultural norms, and shifts within those norms, greatly affect how we weigh the merits of our colleagues' behavior, ideas, and preferences.[36]

Cultural shifts in attitudes, values, and acceptable practices that once took decades or centuries, now mirror more closely the speed of technological advancements.

Consider the following fairly recent culture shifts:

Consider that in 1975, the median age at first marriage for men was 23.5 years and 21.1 years for women, whereas in 2024 it was 30.2 years for men and 28.6 years for women.[37]

Consider that it wasn't until The Equal Credit Opportunity Act was enacted in 1975 that women in the U.S. could get a credit card without a male signature.

Consider that the Civil Rights Act wasn't signed until 1964. This is legislation outlawing discrimination based on race, color, religion, sex, or national origin, and enforcing desegregation of schools and public places.

Consider smoking. In 1980 33.2% of the U.S. adult population smoked cigarettes, compared to 11.6% in 2022.[38]

Consider that in 1995, just under 13% of U.S. adults had a cell phone, where today it's 98%, and over 90% have a smartphone. In 2011 only 35% of cellphone users had smartphones.[39]

I could keep on listing the litany of changes in U.S. culture, from religion and politics to technological changes to obesity and depression rates, but I won't. Suffice it to say, there have been a great many shifts in American culture and many more minor ones just in the last decade.

Depending on your age and experience, the changes may feel unsettling or even like whiplash. What was once socially acceptable/normal or unacceptable/abnormal became unacceptable/abnormal or acceptable/normal many times over, with little warning or explanation.

In a workplace, you have people raised with differing social norms and expectations based on many factors, such as region, family of origin, religion, socioeconomics, et al.

If we think people are semi-blank when they show up to work and we will simply mold them into the organization culture, we are misguided.

The social norms and subsequent shifts a person experiences are part of how they see the world, who they are, and how they understand work.

When we try to see people as devoid of backgrounds, we see them out of context and can find them perplexing. We can also, in weaker moments, 'otherize' and minimize them because they see things differently (or, from my perspective, falsely).[40]

Since all people in your organization have experienced shifting cultural norms, consider these questions:[41]

- Given the work we do in this organization, how can we harness the shifts in culture our team members have experienced to innovate and have our message/products/services resonate with our intended audience?
- What can I learn from someone who has experienced more cultural shifts than I have? What do they see that I don't?
- What can I learn from someone who hasn't lived through the cultural shifts that I've experienced? What do they see that I don't?
- While I value (fill in the blank), my colleague appears to value it differently. Why is that? What is their rationale? What opportunities can be found in these differences?

NOTE: In almost all cases, I discourage political and religious conversations at work. These conversations can quickly cause unnecessary discord and are largely inappropriate at work.

Chapter 22: Generational Wars in the Media

"'Snowflakeism' Gen Z hires are easily offended, and not ready for workplace: business leaders"
– New York Post[42]

"Toxic Expectations & Behaviors Of Old-School Bosses No One Puts Up With Anymore"
– Bolde[43]

Imagine, for a moment that there was no social media or sensationalized journalism. If this were the case, would there be these great generational divides we're experiencing at work?

Yes and No

The fact of the matter is that there are general differences between people of different ages. In addition to the basic biological, lifespan, and development differences, there are the unparalleled accelerated cultural and technological changes in the past 100 years we've been thinking about in this book.

There have always been differences and tensions between generations. Today is no different.

But what is different today is that there is money to be made from exploiting and widening these differences.

Also, we no longer primarily learn and see generational differences through our own experiences, but through the multitude of stories we see and share through media conglomerations.

Even if I haven't had negative experiences with people from different generations, I may conclude that I'm the exception. I must be, because the reporting is such that we are expected to believe the typecasting and demonization of different generations as gospel.

But here's the thing with prejudice. If I'm told I ought to be suspicious of colleagues who are older because they are out of touch, then I am more likely to have that assumption based on what I expect rather than what I experience. If I have heard nothing but the repeated mantra that young people just don't want to work, there's a good chance this will bleed over into my interactions with younger workers. Not based on who they are, but on my assumptions of a whole class of people.

Let's do another bit of imagining. Imagine you wake tomorrow to see the script has flipped on this issue. Instead of people complaining about other generations, generational differences are celebrated and sought after.

Story after personal story comes across your feed of how one generation helped the other at work:

- Anita, who is an executive in her 60s, mentored over 100 20-somethings, and they all thanked her for the care and opportunities she gave them.

- Kyle, a 25-year-old social worker, is being praised by his 70-year-old boss for his innovative way of helping more children.
- The CEO of a fortune 100 instituted a mentor and reverse mentoring program that has resulted in reduced turnover, innovation, higher job satisfaction ratings, and increased revenue.

Imagine if the social media videos made in cars where people are crying about treatment at work were because they were supported and not minimized.

Imagine if social media post comments on generation gaps at work encouraged the person who was having a hard time to work *with*, instead of against, the person from another generation.

Imagine these were the stories flooding your social media feeds, TV stories, and print journalism for the next 10 years.

When the media constantly pushes the narrative that there is a fundamental and unbridgeable gulf between generations, and that we ought to stick with and fight for our side (decade?), this is a lopsided lie.

What good does it do anyone to repeat the terrible advice of 'it's you against them?' They are awful *due to their age*, and you are just right.

While there are differences, there are so many more similarities. But similarities aren't all that sexy to talk about. Similarities aren't great for making click-bait headlines.

To counteract the overhyped and disastrous effect of the misreporting of the generational wars at work, consider asking these questions:

- Could we start our own social media trend based on coming together and harnessing age differences for the good of our colleagues and clients?
- How can we benefit from having people of different ages on our team?
- How can we turn the narrative of suspicion based on age, to an opportunity to win in the marketplace?
- How can we use our differences in ages to make this work environment a case study in excellence?
- What are stereotypes we carry about people of other ages? What counter evidence do we have to combat these stereotypes?
- What are the differences between the generations on this team when it comes to the expectations of how we do our work and how we ought to interact with each other?

Chapter 23: Language

From generational slang to generational punctuation, language is a beast.

The very purpose of language, both in symbols and words, is to communicate.

We *want to* communicate effectively. We *need to* communicate effectively to have healthy and solvent businesses.

We trick ourselves into thinking that words and symbols are stable. But they aren't. They are fluid and tied to the whims of culture.

This changing nature of language can leave us feeling uncomfortable. What was at one time a socially acceptable word is now banned in polite society. We laugh at or are scandalized by those using out-of-date terms, knowing (hoping!) we'll never do that.

And here's the thing. 'Culture' is not uniform. What is okay or encouraged in one business might be cause for dismissal at another.

Consider profanity. Some places don't care if you use colorful language. And more than that, sometimes it's the norm and noticed if someone's speech is habitually 'clean.'

Consider the use of personal pronouns: she/her, he/his, them/they, and so on. What a landmine! Even writing about thinking about pronouns are fighting words for some.

I ask someone's gender pronouns and offend some or don't ask–and thereby assume–and offend others.

What do I say about a person who deviates from the homogenous biological 'standard' in mind or body? Disabled? Differently abled? Or do I refuse to notice difference?

There is also the public and private use of language. We want to communicate with people within and outside our circle.

At work, acronyms are used for expediency and as signifiers of competency and alliance.

Consider nicknames, inside jokes, and terms of endearment. These are meant to communicate to a very specific person or persons and are exclusive to and reinforce the specialness of relationships, which are not meant for outsiders.

Then there's the not-too-private language that is specific to professions. If I asked someone about the ontological status of Yellowstone National Forest and their epistemological justification for their answer, many wouldn't understand what I'm asking. The philosopher or philosophically inclined person knows what I'm asking.

This is why it can be tedious to listen to our friends and family talk about their work, insofar as they use industry terminology and we are on the outside. The words are meaningful to them but largely lost on us.

We all know that young people come up with their own words, usually called slang.[44] The young use these words to communicate with each other. Older generations get ahold of these words and use them typically not quite right, and usually to unintentional comedic effect.[45]

Most of these slang words eventually fall by the wayside. The ones that persist get taken into the wider vernacular, getting into the Urban dictionary, with the cream of the crop into the Oxford English Dictionary, which can be used when we play scrabble.

How does this all apply to generational differences at work?

It is important to know words and symbols can be used to include or exclude. A younger worker may not know a certain word because it refers to an obsolete piece of technology or practice, or it's simply not part of their experience yet. And, conversely, an older worker may not be plugged into youth culture or pop culture, and so a slang word or phrase still has an older meaning attached to it for them or no meaning at all.

A healthy work environment uses language to the benefit of all. When people are made fun of or gossiped about because they don't know a term or are using it incorrectly, this is a red flag that either the company or team is lacking in its ability to communicate as well as lacking in basic civility.

To be a functioning team that communicates excellently, consider holding revolving conversations about cultural and industry relevant trends in terms and language, entertaining questions such as:

- Are there any words we are using that are unclear or out of date, either industry wide or culturally?
- Do we have a document that is updated regularly and is easily accessible to new employees containing both company and industry acronyms?
- Has anyone heard a colleague use an unfamiliar term or acronym?
- Has anyone noticed a colleague using language incorrectly, such as using all caps or too many exclamation points?
- What changes in culture impact the way we communicate with each other, such as changes and updates to emojis and punctuation?
- What, if any, changes in language might be useful to adopt to continue moving forward?
- When communicating with our stakeholders, is anyone aware of updated terminology we can use to communicate more effectively?
- Whose job is it to keep the team up to date on language use?

Chapter 24: Job Duties, aka *That's Not My Job*

I once worked where there was a question as to who was supposed to clean the microwave in the breakroom. Many emails were sent over a long period of time. As it turned out, there were differing expectations as to who should be tasked with the microwave's upkeep.

This is a common theme. Job duties, and the scope of individual responsibilities, are often unclear.

- Is it my job to pick up trash as I walk into the building?
- Is it my job to be on call during weekends?
- Is it my job to pick up the slack when the company downsizes workers but not the work?

There are the unspoken job duty expectations that are used to judge ourselves and our colleagues as to whether we/they are preforming well.

For example, some people believe that everyone should start at the bottom of an organization before they are allowed to move up. The idea that 'everyone should have to start out like I did.' That's how business works.

- If I started out as a 21-year-old college grad getting coffee for the senior staff, so should you.
- If I had to work nights and weekends as a young professional, so should you.

- If I had to do the filing or start in the mailroom, so should you.

Everyone should start at the bottom. Grunt work and less than savory jobs are the gig. Everyone starts this way. This is only fair.

There are also the unarticulated standards of professionalism, with the expectation to take care of the company through actions. *I owe this company my loyalty, which works itself out by going above and beyond my job description. I should:*

- At all times roll up my sleeves and help colleagues out
- Only say good things about my employer publicly
- Pick up the stray piece of trash I see
- Stay until the wee early morning hours to finish the project

My job is the actual work I do, plus the all-encompassing 'and duties as assigned.' Of course, I will help and do what is needed.

These 'duties as assigned'[46] are a sticking point for many of the younger generation. They come to work, do their work, and still meet resistance or complaints from older team members because they aren't doing more.

But what is this more?

- Why are these unexplained duties up to me to discover?
- What about work/life boundaries?
- How do I ensure that this job doesn't creep up and take over my life? My job doesn't love me, but my family and friends do.

When you have multiple generations working together, there are bound to be different understandings of who should be doing what and when. Luckily, there is an easy solution: *Dialogue*.

Ask questions, such as:

- If I'm feeling something being asked of me is unprofessional, for example getting coffee for my boss, how should this be addressed?
- If someone on the team is doing so-called 'grunt' work like getting the coffee orders or cleaning the office kitchen, has it been explained as to why this is one of their duties? Are these appropriate duties?
- On this team, what are the different work expectations for those who are salaried vs. those who are non-exempt? How does this designation get made and what are the kinds of differences likely to be reflected in what a person is expected to do based on this designation?
- What are best practices right now that will help our company, team, and individuals reach their goals?

- What are the number of expected working hours, on average? How should each person think about and arrange her/his time when they work more than the average?
- What duties can I turn down?
- What duties should I say yes to?
- What is the match between the job description and the actual job?
- What kinds of changes should we make (if any) to the current distribution of labor on our team?
- What kinds of tasks should we say 'no' to because they really aren't part of our job and take away from getting our work done?
- What kinds of things usually come up that are not a typical part of our jobs, but we should do?
- When is the last time the team discussed division of labor and the reasons behind it?

Chapter 25: Who's in Charge

If you think about company culture in the mid-twentieth century, the dominant leadership style was command and control with a strict pecking order and hierarchy based largely on seniority, sex (male), race (white), and an overall palpable deference to authority.

This way of thinking about the authority structure at work has ramifications for how work gets done. The boss is to be appeased. Collaboration is allowed, but through an elaborate dance where the authority structure is acknowledged and attended to. This is the art, dance, and game of sucking-up.

This way of thinking about company culture has been hanging on into the 21st century; and unfortunately, is still found in many institutions.

This means you have many people in the workforce where this kind of thinking and leadership structure are normal.

The boss, Miranda, in the movie *The Devil Wears Prada*, is an example of this type of leadership. The movie shows this leadership style to be inhumane and mocked by those around her and yet admired because Miranda gets things done.

The kind of fear, awe, and wide berth given to Miranda is mirrored in many workplaces. When the boss is around, we pretend. The real work and conversations happen when the threat (the boss) is tucked away in her/his corner office.

What do we have here? Rule by title and a lack of transparency, where looking the part is more important than a cascading healthy work environment for all.

If you are of an older demographic at work, Command and Control leadership style is all too familiar and relatively normal. To many younger workers, collaboration and a decline in the insistence that we ought to defer to those who are older is the expectation.

The idea that all colleagues have something valuable to contribute, and therefore, ought to be listened to is the message younger generations are exposed to and expect. Gone is the adage that the young should be seen and not heard. Cooperation and collaboration are stressed in classrooms from pre-K to graduate school.

Who should be heard at work? Everyone, regardless of age. This is the expectation of people entering the workforce in 2025.

If I think speaking up is earned and you think speaking up is a right given when hired, unnecessary conflict is bound to set in.

Since you have different generations on your team, and in your organization, ask questions, such as:

- How does the authority structure really work in the everyday running of the business?
- Why is this style the best way to work excellently, promote high engagement, and a healthy work environment?
- Does my understanding of authority structures at work, or how I think they 'should' be, reflect the actual practice where I work?
- What do those leadership styles entail when it comes to authority distribution, autonomy in decision-making, and speaking up in meetings and elsewhere?
- What are the leadership styles of the CEO and manager of your team?
- What, specifically, does each worker have control over, and what should be asked? For example: do I tell my boss I'm taking vacation days, or do I ask permission for vacation days?

Section IV: Dismantling the Two Biggest Generational Workplace Myths

Chapter 26: Young People Don't Want to Work

Meet your newest colleague, Brit. She's 22 years old and graduated college 6 months ago.

Based on the tiny bit of information you have, answer the following questions:

1. What kind of worker do you think Brit will be?

2. What would surprise you about Brit's work ethic?

3. What kind of behavior do you expect from her?

4. Before you turn the page and learn more, why is this your expectation of Brit?

Here is more information about Brit:

She was born after Y2K and 9/ll. The world of work for her, since her first job at a national grocery chain, has involved the world of computers.

She's always had access to the internet, computers, and cell phones. Speaking of phones, her mom is still enabled to track Brit's phone. And before you ask, she played soccer growing up in a community youth soccer league and always received participation trophies.

Brit grew up going out to eat regularly, and with the idea that mental health is important. This idea was regularly reinforced through her public education.

Brit's mom was a working-class real estate agent for a national firm who lost her job in the 2008 recession. Since then, the family has never been the same financially.

Brit was better than the average student and joined the university student government as a senator in her sophomore year, and did a travel study the summer before her senior year. She worked on and off as a work study while in college and the grocery store during the summers.

Brit is a relatively average 22-year-old.

And now she is working in your office.

Why do you think she's going to have a poor work ethic?

How should younger workers act?

If younger workers have poor work ethics and are entitled, where did that come from? Did they give it to themselves? Or is this even true about this whole class of people? And why do the young, since as far back as forever, have this reputation?

This is a very old sentiment.

The ancient Roman poet Horace, in the first Century BCE said, "'Our sires' age was worse than 'our grandsires.' We, their sons, are more worthless than they; so in our turn we shall give the world a progeny yet more corrupt." *Horace, Odes, Book III, Ode 6.*

Each generation, rightly or wrongly, thinks that their times were harder than the times the youth live in. The result: pampered, entitled, and idle youth.

Would you like more modern proof?

Paul Fairie is credited with this 130-year newspaper compilation cry of "nobody wants to work anymore."[47]

"NOBODY WANTS TO WORK ANY MORE!"

A brief history of capitalists complaining that nobody wants to work for starvation wages

2022 — According to a new survey released by TinyPulse, 1 in 5 executive leaders agree with this statement: "No one wants to work". These same leaders cite a "lack of response to job

2014 — What has happened to the work ethic in America? Nobody wants to work anymore. It has not always been that way. When I first started to work as a teenager, I saw people work hard.

2006 — like nobody wants to work anymore and when they do

1999 — "Nobody wants to work anymore," Cecil said. "They all want to work in

1981 — off this land last week. But they just fooled around. They didn't want to work. Nobody wants to work anymore.

1979 — "Nobody wants to work anymore."

— disgusted businessman

1969 — called "Nobody Wants to Work Anymore." Talking about un-

1952 — everybody was getting too darned lazy and nobody wants to work anymore. That's the truth if I ever heard it.

1940 — trouble is everybody is on relief or a pension — nobody wants to work anymore."

1937 — ams counties are complaining that "Nobody wants to work anymore." There is work, it is reported, for 15

1922 — it is because nobody wants to work any more unless they can

1916 — he answered, "the reason for food scarcity is that nobody wants to work as hard as they used to. I asked a

1905 — unreliable. None want to work for wages.

1894 — next winter? It is becoming apparent that nobody wants to work these hard times.

Here are a few more quotes to add to the list:

1882

"The old people, as a rule, work well, but the younger generation are fond of leisure and find a ready excuse for idleness...."[48]

1936

"Too many times the younger generation has been blamed for irresponsibility, pettiness, idleness, and many other apparent faults. Older folks eye the younger ones with scorn."[49]

1963

"Kids! I don't know what's wrong with these kids today! Kids! Who can understand anything they say? Kids! They are disobedient, disrespectful oafs! Noisy, crazy, sloppy, lazy, loafers!"[50]

1990

"They have trouble making decisions. They would rather hike in the Himalayas than climb a corporate ladder. They have few heroes, no anthems, no style to call their own. They crave entertainment, but their attention span is as short as one zap of a TV dial. They hate yuppies, hippies and druggies. They postpone marriage because they dread divorce. They sneer at Range Rovers, Rolexes and red suspenders. What they hold dear are family life, local activism, national parks, penny loafers and mountain bikes. They possess only a hazy sense of their own identity but a monumental preoccupation with all the problems the preceding generation will leave for them to fix."[51]

1993

"Well, enough is enough. As a baby boomer, I'm fed up with the ceaseless carping of a handful of spoiled, self-indulgent, overgrown adolescents. Generation Xers may like to call themselves the "Why Me?" generation, but they should be called the "Whiny" generation. If these pusillanimous purveyors of pseudo-angst would put as much effort into getting a life as they do into writing about their horrible fate, we'd be spared the weekly diatribes that pass for reasoned argument in newspapers and magazines."[52]

2013

"I am about to do what old people have done throughout history: call those younger than me lazy, entitled, selfish and shallow."[53]

2025

"If millennials and their successors, the so-called Gen-Zs, want to get ahead, maybe it's time to stop complaining and start changing."[54]

You see, this is a tale as old as time. The cry that the young just don't want to work, and if they do they will come with an entitled and poor work ethic, is an insult hurled against younger generations decade after decade, ad infinitum.

What, then, is really going on?

Change

Society changes.

Expectations shift.

The world you were born into is not the world your children are/will be born into.

As you get older, you collect experiences and change.

Memories are faulty.

Change can be hard.

I can feel some people looking for what's missing from this list, saying, "No, really, Merry. You obviously don't get it. These 20 somethings just are terrible workers. The world has undergone such a radical shift that we have actually managed to bring about a generation (or two) of cry babies who are weak, unrealistic, and need everything spoon fed to them."

No.

Labeling generations as weak and entitled is the path towards distance, not community. This is not the way toward building a healthy work environment.

This way of thinking is self-indulgent and lets leaders and managers off the hook of doing their job, which is leading and managing.

Yesterday, I was having a conversation with someone I'd just met at a local business event. I mentioned I was writing a book about generation gaps. This person, we'll call her Janet, has managed people for decades. She told me she used to be able to tell an employee what to do, and they'd just do it. Now, the younger employees need to be told why to do something, not just to do it.

I'm not certain what Janet was expecting from me, but I nodded my head because I know about this trend of younger workers wanting to know not only *what* they are to do, but the *why* behind it.

While Janet's tone intimated this was a bad development, this request of 'why' seems not only reasonable to me, but something, it turns out, lots of employees of all ages want to know: not just what to do, but why to do it.

But this *is* a change, and change can feel like something has gone wrong.

To embrace the fact of change instead of bemoaning it is to win in the world of business. The social contract shifts over time. So, either keep up or spin your wheels, pining for a time that is lost, thereby losing out on the opportunities in front of you.

Taking this example, let's suppose the trend of younger workers wanting to know the 'why' of a work task is a turn for the worse; what should be done about it?

Dialogue

- Clearly communicate expectations to all staff members

- Offer relevant and comprehensive training
- Make reasonable adjustments

If you are one of the younger generations at work, how can you combat this narrative that you and your generational cohorts have a terrible work ethic?

If you are one of the older generations at work, how can you combat the knee jerk reaction to label a younger colleague's work ethic as lacking, and instead get curious about information or assistance they may need to be successful?

Chapter 27: Older Workers are Out of Touch

Meet Stephen. Stephen is an advertising executive on a business trip. The year is 1985.

Midflight, he falls asleep. Upon arrival, he's awakened by a flight attendant. Stretching, he notices the people around him look slightly off, dressed a bit funny, and everyone is looking down at a thin black rectangle box that's emitting light.

You guessed it. Stephen has time traveled to the year 2026.

Imagine Stephen going into his office. He's used an Apple 2E computer and a ginormous cell phone, but he's never:

- Had a laptop
- Sent an email
- Gone through a windows update
- Heard of or used social media
- Used a deck/PowerPoint for a presentation
- Used the internet
- Had a Zoom meeting

Consider Stephen's world, his references, and what he knows to be normal and standard business practices. Plopping him down in 2025, a mere 40 years into the future, doesn't change everything. Let's refrain from being that dramatic. But the changes in culture and workplace culture are extensive.

Stephen is a relic. Do you want him working on your ad campaign? Do you want him as your boss? Did I mention he smokes in the office?

Does this mean Stephen is useless, and has no good ideas? Absolutely not. But how would you treat Stephen at work? What would you think of his abilities?

Stephen, understandably, is out of touch.

What if we changed Stephen's profession. What if we made him a heart surgeon, air traffic controller, or travel agent?[55]

It doesn't really matter what profession he is in, there's going to be a learning curve to get him work-ready in 2025; not only in the subject matter, but also in the way in which work gets done, along with expectations of what it means to be a good colleague and boss.

As people progress in their career, they keep up to date in their fields, or risk getting left behind. Many credentialing professions require continuing education hours to maintain the credential.

Older workers are not relics. In fact, many older workers have the most knowledge and stay more current and up to date on trends in their industries due to their connections and their broad view of their industry given their experiences.

So, what's the problem? Why do people from older generations get labeled 'out of touch?'

We tend to generalize. When someone is friendly to us, we tend to see them as friendly. When someone doesn't show up to a few meetings, we categorize them as unreliable.

So, when I have a conversation with my older colleague who is dressed from a different time, uses old-fashioned words, doesn't know how Instagram works, and uses emojis incorrectly, I generalize this person is out of touch. They are operating in an outdated and phased out operating system. Much like using AOL Online has disappeared, so is their waning relevance.

Given this kind of generalization, it can feel as if older colleagues are just like Stephen from the thought experiment, stuck in a perpetual time warp.

Is this a fair assessment?

No.

What reasons are the younger generations given for **not** making this assessment, given the narrative the older generations have made about them? If I feel like my older colleagues have a general disdain for me and my generation, why should I extend grace to them? If they're going to call me names and make no attempt to understand me in my particularity, why should I try to understand them? They are stuck in their ways, holding back innovation.

Younger workers are mirroring the unhelpful rhetoric leveled against them.

Being an older worker doesn't make you irrelevant, anymore that being a younger worker qualifies you as relevant. Being relevant, an asset, and professional is entirely about how each person chooses to show up at work. Being respectful, coachable, curious, and a life-long learner has nothing to do with age.

If you are one of the older generations at work, how can you combat this narrative that you and your generational cohorts are irrelevant?

- Use the power of dialogue.
- Listen. Listen to real concerns.
- Refrain from repeating the untrue talking point 'the younger generation doesn't want to work anymore.' Imagine you were in your 20s and you heard your older colleagues, boss, and boss' boss repeat this refrain over and over. Wouldn't you get the hint that you are not welcomed, valued, or seen?
- Be coachable, engaged, and keep your knowledge and skills in your line of work up to date.

Section V: Tips to Win the Culture Wars at Work

Chapter 28: Curiosity

Being curious is one of the greatest assets to possess.

When you're curious:

- You are less likely to react and rush to judgement.
- You are more likely to pause and consider what's really going on: what's working and what's not, how to improve it, and whether/how to fix it.

Being a good colleague requires self-reflection and accurate self-assessment. If you've ever read a leadership book, you know self-reflection is a necessary condition to be a great leader. But, if you're not a very reflective person, how do you become one?

Intentionally developing the muscle of curiosity about what's going on around you will be beneficial as you strive to become self-reflective.

Here's a simple exercise you can do to develop your curiosity – play devil's advocate. This involves taking something you believe and coming up with counter arguments.[56]

Having a curious demeanor requires paying attention to what's going on inside and outside of you.

- Why are we doing this instead of that?
- Why did I say that?
- Why did they do that?

These reflective questions are not about second guessing yourself and others. They're about being present, paying attention, and gathering information to make better decisions. Curiosity, when honed, is a sign of confidence.

When it comes to the generation wars at work, consider these curiosity inducing questions:

- Are there any generational differences here? If so, what are they?
- How can we benefit from generational differences?
- What should we be watching for that could turn generational differences into a threat to having a healthy work environment?
- Have I asked others I work with if they have experienced any negative impact attributed to generational differences? If so, what is the issue/s?
- How can we work together to turn generational issues into a win for ourselves, colleagues, company, and clients?
- How have you benefited from working with colleagues in different generations? Ask the same questions, but of your colleagues. How have they benefited?
- How do you address generational differences where you work? What mechanisms do you have to spot them, talk about them, and ensure those differences turn into wins for your organization instead of a series of unnecessary battles?

- How do your clients benefit from the diversity of age in your organization?
- What are the challenges you face when it comes to generational differences? What are your preferences that others may not prefer, which is tied to the generation you are from?

What organizational system, policy, procedure, or ritual will you put in place to support curiosity at work?

Chapter 29: Practicing the Golden Rule

Treat others the way you want to be treated.

We want others to treat us fairly and with respect and kindness. When this doesn't happen, we disengage and workplaces are on their way to becoming a toxic mess.

When it comes to generational differences, how can this universal golden rule be applied?

When you feel annoyed with a colleague, and you attribute this behavior to their age:

- Stop and pause
- Say out loud to yourself what you were just thinking by:
  - → Naming the behavior
  - → Saying what you think is causing the behavior

Frank isn't listening to me because he thinks younger workers like me have nothing important to say. O.K. Boomer!

Or

Alisa isn't listening to me because she doesn't have any respect for seniority. That's just like all Gen Z!

- Get curious and examine your age-based conclusions
  - → Notice that not all people from a group act the same way. Just as you don't want to be judged by a detached standard of an age

range you happen to fall into, don't do this to your colleagues.

→ Get specific about the problematic or bothersome behavior and then ask your colleague what's going on.

"Frank, I noticed when I spoke in the meeting today and last Wednesday, you didn't acknowledge what I said. What's going on?"

"Alisa, when we were making the vacation schedule, you said seniority shouldn't matter. Let's talk about this. Why do you think seniority shouldn't be considered?"

When it comes to avoiding unnecessary drama and tension at work, and instead, bringing about a healthy work environment, treat your colleagues as unique individuals.

In this way you are treating others in a way that respects who they are, and how you want to be treated – as you, and not as a nameless, faceless group.

What organizational system, policy, procedure, or ritual will you put in place to support treating colleagues according to the golden rule at work?

Chapter 30: Continually Set and Assess Expectations

Expectations are mighty and important. The right set of expectations sets you, your team, and organization up for success. On the other hand, misplaced expectations are a recipe for disaster.

Unaligned expectations are a cause of many generational issues at work.

I have one set of expectations given my work history and experience, and you have a different set.

Since **you know** how easy it is to miscommunicate and not be on the same page, it is in your best interest to continually set and assess workplace expectations.

This way, current team members know what's required of them, what the standards are, and have a say in what standards are or are not working. And as teams are fluid, if you are in the habit of having expectation conversations, this is a great way for new colleagues to really get a feel for how work is done here, and what is valued.

It is unreasonable to think what was expected of a worker 10, 5, or even 2 years ago holds true today, from the employee, employer, and marketplace.

Change is the name of the game. Being in the habit of having **ongoing dialogues** surrounding setting and assessing workplace expectations is an excellent way to normalize and accept change while also not being blindsided by differing generational expectations.

Have everyone on your team answer the following questions:

- Who's in charge?
- Who makes decisions about what?
- What does excellence look like?
- When is 'good enough' great?
- What is the expectation for dealing with conflict?
- What is the best way to communicate with every member of my team and the team as a whole?
- How are wins communicated?
- How are issues communicated?
- What expectations does a colleague have when they think something is wrong or not working?
- What is the path for promotions and raises?
- What is the mission of the organization?
- What does it mean to be on time?
- What are 10 specific behaviors that are considered best practice here?
- What are 3 outdated workplace practices here?
- What are the greatest strengths of your team?
- What threats does your team face when it comes to the current members of the team (for example: short-handed, gaps in knowledge, etc.)?

What organizational system, policy, procedure, or ritual will you put in place to continually set and assess expectations at work?

Chapter 31: Setting and Resetting Civility Standards

Just as a healthy workplace sets and assesses workplace expectations, organizations and teams should have civility standards.

What is a civility standard? I'm glad you asked! A standard of civility is the way in which you are expected to treat and be treated by your colleagues.

It's not enough to say, 'Be Professional' because this means different things to different people.

Start by determining three to five employee-centric values, as determined largely by the employees, not just the C-suite. Once you've determined your values, get specific and clear.[57]

Let's try this.

Meet Company ABC. They have gone through the process of determining their employee-centric values and have landed on Communication, Integrity, and Meaningful Work.

Part of determining the employee-centric values involves defining what the word means for them in their organization, along with examples and counterexamples of the value at work.

Value #1: Communication

Definition: A commitment to clear, consistent, open, and honest communication, where collaboration, listening, and being listened to is the standard expected practice.

Examples:

- Communicating schedules: knowing who's where; what's on the calendar; who's late; etc.

- Communicating issues as they arise

- Respecting co-workers' input and everyone's point of view and contributions

- Respecting co-workers' privacy

What to avoid:

- Interrupting when someone is speaking

- Not listening

- Being unaware of other people's input

- Gossiping

Value #2: Integrity

Definition: Treating all people with dignity and respect, demonstrating trustworthiness, self-reflection, and operating with a high work ethic.

Examples:

- Following through on promises

- Always doing the right thing, even when people aren't watching

- Reflecting on good and bad past events and experiences to improve future events and behaviors

- Expecting good in others

What to avoid:

- Micromanaging others

- Getting into other people's business

- Gossiping and stirring up drama

- Doing the bare minimum at work

Value #3: Meaningful Work

Definition: Engaging in mission driven, impactful work that both encourages all employees to find work/life balance and supports continual professional growth.

Examples:

- Keeping up with your schedule and managing time at work. So, it's clear when you should and shouldn't be working.

- Participating in continual development through attending conferences, workshops, community events, reading, etc.

- Coming to work when you're healthy, being prepared/ready to work, and being mission minded.

What to avoid:

- Acting counter to Company ABC's mission

- Meddling in other people's work/life balance

- Stagnation and refusal to try new things - 'this is the way we've always done it' thinking

- Going to work when sick or unable to do your work. - If physically sick, too tired, etc., you should take a sick or vacation day.

Great work, Company ABC! But as we know, the work is not done. It has just begun. Now these values need to be lived out every day, reinforced, and periodically reviewed to see if they need to be updated.

Being committed to a healthy work environment means holding real dialogues when a colleague demonstrates a gap in behavior or performance.

Colleagues knowing what the standards of behavior are and that there are normalized mechanisms for addressing gaps is the path towards establishing and maintaining a healthy work environment.

This will also serve to eliminate ageism on your team. When age-related differences present themselves – and **they will** – if you have established modes of communication to notice differences and talk about them, everyone wins.

It is so much easier to address a gap in someone's behavior when it first happens, rather than months or years later when the behavior has become entrenched and destructive.

Don't let this happen to your team. The different generations on your team **are** an asset. Don't let the neglect of establishing and enforcing civility standards cause your downfall.

What organizational system, policy, procedure, or ritual will you put in place to set and reset civility standards at work?

Chapter 32: Normalize Difference

It is common to see and value the ideas, technology, activities, and pop culture based on the generation in which you grew up.

While having different preferences is normal, we win at work when we prize the unique and individual insights and expertise our colleagues bring. This means we ought to expect not to see eye-to-eye in all areas.

If this is a new expectation – expecting and valuing difference – then how can you, your team, and your organization prepare for and normalize differences at work?

Learn, Practice, Value, and Insist on Disagreeing Well

Since there will be disagreements, decide to navigate them in a manner that, instead of harming people through the process of a conflict, encourages people to speak up.

Learning to disagree well involves the ability to talk about challenging ideas without degrading and disrespecting those in the conversation.

Learning to disagree well is vital if you want to win the generation wars.

Leaders

How are you to do this? If you are the leader, periodically verbalize this expectation:

"Because we are different people and come from different backgrounds, experiences, and generations, we will disagree with each other. This is normal. We should expect disagreement."

And/or

"I take civil disagreement as a sign of engagement and creativity."

And/or

"Everyone should expect to disagree with each other from time to time. This has happened and will happen. We are, therefore, going to learn how to disagree well with each other."

And/or

"If no one is ever disagreeing with the ideas offered, something is wrong. I don't want 'group think.' Always agreeing is a sign of either needing to diversify our hires, disengagement, and/or bad management."

And/or

"We will disagree over smaller issues, such as what temperature to set the office thermostat, and bigger issues, such as the direction of a campaign, distribution of resources, and promotions. Whether the issue is big or small, all issues can cause harm to a work environment if left unaddressed. Therefore, you are expected to speak up when there is an issue in a professional manner."

Leaders, put your money where your mouths are and support your team, because most people don't know how to speak up at work when they feel threatened or there is a power imbalance.

Since this **is true**, provide resources to help your colleagues navigate circumstances they find difficult. A wonderful resource is having an organizational ombuds[58] office. An ombuds is a conflict management specialist who focuses on assisting people to solve their own problems.

Imagine you're 23 and having an issue with a colleague who is 65. You find their jokes off-putting, and sometimes offensive. They talk down to you. What do you do?

If you are not skilled in holding difficult conversations, you may do nothing to solve the problem. You might leave your job. You may find comfort in talking to your colleagues about this person, which usually turns into gossip. Gossip can easily turn into factions and/or minimizing someone. Whichever way this goes, these options do not lean towards having healthy work environments.

If the goal is to **learn to disagree well**, we must pay attention to the *learn* part in the sentence. Holding difficult conversations is a learned skill. It must be encouraged, practiced, and honed.

Since this is the case, have resources to help your employees develop and learn how to manage conflicts well and hold productive difficult conversations.

Employees

It is your job to be professional. This means accepting that your colleagues will think and act differently from you. You can choose to bemoan difference or accept it as reality and decide to make it into an asset.

It is your job to speak up. No one can read your mind.[59] So many times, we think people know they are bothering us, intentionally annoying us, or getting in our way, but this is rarely the case. Most people see themselves as the hero, the best worker. Since people don't know they are bothering you, or the extent to which there is an issue, it is up to you to speak up if there is a problem.

The sooner you speak up, the easier it is to address the issue. The longer you let it go, the more damage is caused.

If you need assistance developing your skills to speak up, read a book, take a class, watch a video, get a conflict coach, find a mentor, etc. Do something! No one else can do this for you.

1. Accept there will be differences with others that you will find difficult to deal with.
2. Develop skills to hold difficult conversations.
3. Hold difficult conversations.
4. Repeat on loop for the rest of your life.

What organizational system, policy, procedure, or ritual will you put in place normalizing the expectation and acceptance of difference at work?

Chapter 33: Consider Their Perspective

You are about to see a picture of the most important cat who is currently living.

Consider the claim I'm making.

The. Most. Important. Living. Cat.

Before you turn the page to glimpse this incredible cat, what do you think are the qualifications for being the most important living cat?

With your list of qualifications in mind, you are ready to see him.

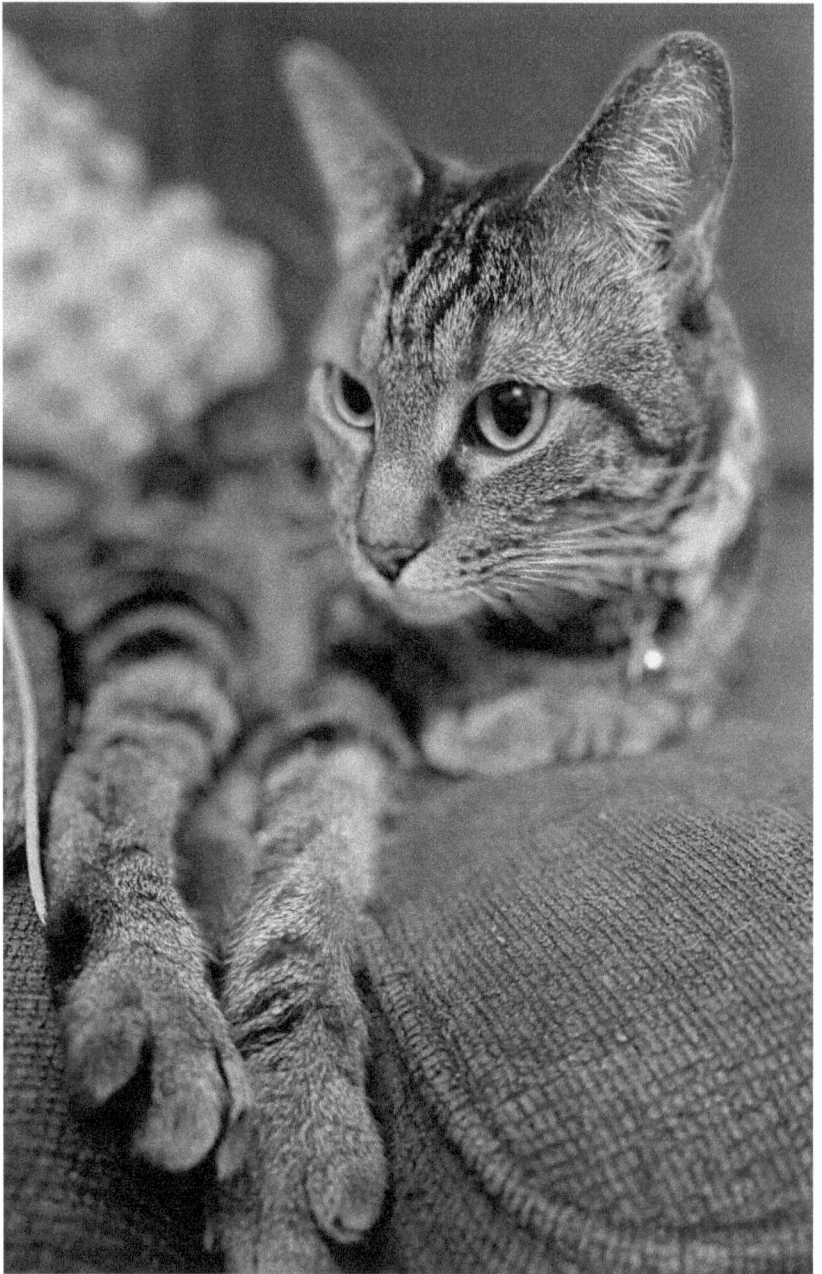

Of course it's Ronan! Who else would I choose?

Ronan is the most important living cat, from my perspective, because he is the most impactful cat I know.

Ronan is universally adored by anyone who meets him. He has his own Instagram account, which was started early in the pandemic. But these are not the reasons he's the most important.[60]

He's the most important cat because I love him. My kids and husband love him. When one of my children comes home, the first thing they do is seek out Ronan.

I could site evidence of the ways in which he is a remarkable cat, but even after hearing it all laid out before you, I doubt you'll agree. I know you don't think he's the best, and I understand.

Look at him again. What do you see? You probably see a 2-dimensional picture of a handsome gentleman. But love him? Think he's the most important living cat?

When I tell you Ronan really is the most important living cat; I'm telling you the truth. He is ... to me and my family, and he's not the most important living cat to you. Why should he be?

And that's the point. The conflict I am in, the pain I feel, the loss or uncertainty I experience due to changes at work may look irrelevant to you, inconsequential, and even small. They might be irrelevant, inconsequential, and small to you, because you don't see what I see. You don't value the same things in the same ways I do, and therefore we have a choice.

The choice is to:

1. Minimize our colleagues and ridicule them because they care about things that are silly. They are 'silly' or 'petty' because they seem trivial to us. When our colleagues trivialize what we think is important, this encourages factions, lack of innovation, lower workplace engagement, and higher turnover.

   Or

2. We can open a dialogue. Listen to their perceptions, desires, and needs. Discuss industry and organizational standards, looking for the best combination of addressing real needs to improve engagement, higher productivity, and winning in the marketplace.

If someone is telling you about their Most Important Living Cat (MILC), listen to them. They are telling you important information about what's going right or wrong for them. This is about them, their MILC, not about yours. Listen, come along side, and see what can be adjusted.

In generational speak, the MILC could be about anything. Let go of what your ideas of 'what should be' as the only legitimate and most important ideas and embrace the reality of different perspectives.

There are a multiplicity of ideas, beliefs, and desires on your team and in your organization. Someone's MILC and/or the issue they have is secondary to how to treat them. Treat your colleagues as individuals. Treat them excellently. Listen, learn, and collaborate with them.

What organizational system, policy, procedure, or ritual will you put in place to encourage coworkers to consider different perspectives at work?

Chapter 34: Mentor and Reverse Mentor

A mentor is a trusted advisor.

We usually think of a mentor to mentee relationship as the experienced person coming along side of and investing in someone who is new to the field.

The mentor invests in the mentee, showing them the ropes. Pointing out potential pitfalls and opportunities, the mentor is a reliable source of information and guidance.

A traditional mentoring relationship is a great professional development opportunity for both parties to learn and grow.

While I wholeheartedly encourage mentoring in this traditional way, I also encourage reverse mentoring. Reverse mentoring is as it sounds, a younger worker[61] mentors the experienced colleague in areas such as:

- Their expectations regarding pay, office culture, and work/life balance. [62]
- What they learned in school/training about the profession, such as what is currently being taught as 'best practices.'
- What they care about when it comes to the vision and mission of the organizations they work with.
- What they consider excellent leadership to be.

- What they've experienced as exceeding their expectations regarding working in this organization and team.
- What they were surprised at in this organization and team.
- What has been difficult so far.
- What team and organizational practices they consider out-of-date.
- What they think could be improved upon.
- What they enjoy the most at work.

Mentoring is a fabulous way to get dialogue flowing between colleagues, and since proximity is a great way to combat ageism, mentoring and reverse-mentoring is an excellent path towards building strong, internal networks.

What organizational system, policy, procedure, or ritual will you put in place for mentoring and reverse mentoring at work?

Chapter 35: Hold Targeted Topic Sessions

"Merry, adding another meeting or agenda item to the bloated agenda? Are you kidding me?"

Hear me out. Regularly talking about the health and climate of the work environment is an important, low cost, simple, and sustainable measure to maintain a healthy work environment.

It's easy, over the weeks and months, to not think about how the team interacts daily. Typically, by the time whatever is going wrong reaches the ears of the boss, damage has already been done.

Loosely summarized, the second law of thermodynamics states that without intervention, everything is in the process of falling apart.

If you are not intentionally, habitually, and systematically working on the health of your work culture, it will naturally tend towards chaos.

To counteract this tendency, what do you think might happen if you intentionally took time to ask team culture questions before or after a meeting? What if instead of everyone saying one 'fun fact' about themselves or recapping what they did over the weekend, a specific culture question was asked?

You could let the team know ahead of time what the question of the week is and keep a Google doc where people can add their own questions.

You could use a book such as *How to Be Unprofessional at Work: Tips to Ensure Failure*, which has 80 'tips' of what **not** to do at work, and start a conversation about what to do instead to bring about and maintain a healthy work environment.[63]

Instead of or in addition to adding items to the meeting agenda, carve out time for 'Let's work together' sessions, with work culture topics such as:

- A 'start, stop, continue' session
- An 'articulation' session
- A 'what has changed' session
- A 'what I wish I had known' session
- A 'review of the onboarding experience' session
- A 'what's new in culture' session
- A 'what I see resonating with people my age' session
- A 'what my other company got right' session
- A 'what my other company got wrong' session
- A 'what's the status of social media trends' session
- A 'what's our demographic and do we reflect it' session
- A 'team blind spot' session

Imagine thinking and talking about your team and company culture regularly. There would be little room for misunderstandings and conflicts rooted in generational gaps that go unnoticed and in turn become unmanaged.

When we identify issues early, we can use that knowledge to build a stronger foundation, access new ideas, harness creativity and build stronger and more engaged team members.

Or

We can ignore differences, not talking about shifting culture norms, ideas, preferences, leaving us open to unmanaged conflicts, and losing out both monetarily and humanly.

The bottom line is this: healthy work cultures rarely occur on their own. It takes sustained, intentional effort to bring them about and maintain them.

And this is a hard fact: if you do not have a plan to address workplace conflicts early, often, swiftly, and justly, you are being irresponsible with company resources, and setting money and people on fire.[64]

What organizational system, policy, procedure, or ritual will you put in place to hold regular targeted topic sessions at work?

Chapter 36: Onboarding Practices

What was your first day at work like at your current job? How long did the onboarding process take and what did it consist of?

Some are shown to their desk and told to jump right in on day one. For others, the onboarding process is filled with months of learning particular systems, laws, and practices and they don't start to work on the job until months later when all the training is completed.

Once onboarded, the behavioral expectations and standards usually aren't articulated. Sure, there may be a handbook that contains the codes of conduct and what happens if you violate them. And you may be told where to voice any concerns.

Whatever the process was for you, it's very rare to find an organization that tells new hires about the **practical** day-to-day social expectations**.**

Every organization and every team operates with the stated norms *and* unstated norms. For example, your place of employment may close for an hour at noon for lunch. This may be the stated policy, but the *actual practice* and expectation might be:

- Everyone eats at their desk, working through the lunch hour.
- Everyone eats together in the break room or goes out together most days.

- Only taking 30 minutes is the expectation.
- Nobody cares or watches what you do for lunch or how long you take.

Or consider what time to arrive at work. You're told to be at work every day at 8 a.m. But what is the unspoken expectation?

- It could be 7:30 a.m. or 7:45 a.m.
- 8 a.m. means 8 a.m. on the dot!
- As long as it's just a few minutes after 8 a.m., that's fine.
- As long as you're there by 8:30 a.m. you're fine.
- No one is watching and no one cares what time you come in or leave if your work is getting done.

There are the stated rules the new employee hears and what's *really* expected. Rarely are these two one and the same.

Imagine as part of the onboarding process you had a list of questions for the new person to ask her new team the first week or two.

Your check list may include:

- What are the expected hours, and do they differ depending on role?
- What are 'after hours' work expectations?
- What do people do for lunch?
- What is the dress code (with examples of what is expected and what is a violation)?

- How are meetings handled? How do you make certain you have the right number of meetings – not too few and not too many?
- What is the team email/texting/etc. standard practice? (Do you use emojis? Do you start every email with something like 'I hope all is well' and sign off with a version of 'Warm wishes' or do you prize an economy of words?)
- What behavior gets you promoted?
- What are some team challenges?
- How have you been mentored here?
- What is the promotion process here?
- From your perspective, what does it mean to be a colleague in good standing?

By the end of her first month, have the new hire report during a team meeting what she found out. In addition to the information from her mini team interviews, have her include any questions or observations she has. Make space to notice and discuss (seemingly) contradictory information.[65]

You don't have to wait for a new employee to ask these questions. Since it is easy to slip out of alignment in the normal course of work, this practice not only serves as an opportunity to align team expectations but could also serve as an initiation into your team's new practice of and commitment to ongoing dialogue, and the acceptance that change is part of work.

What organizational system, policy, procedure, or ritual will you put in place to ensure that excellent onboarding consistently occurs?

Chapter 37: Organizational Employee-Centric Culture Summits

Once a year, hold an organizational employee-centric culture summit.

If you are the CEO/President/Boss, you can make this happen for your organization. If you are a team lead/manager, you can make this happen for the people who report to you. If you are a regular employee, you could suggest this to your team leader.[66]

A summit is an opportunity to reflect on, explore, and improve upon the climate of the work environment. Traditionally, summits are reserved for leaders and human resource types, but I say include everyone.

Check in. Take a pause to reflect on and assess what's going on in the organization and what's on the horizon, what's important and why, specifically focusing on the employee experience.

Give everyone a list of questions to fill out and submit ahead of time. Gather all the people in the organization to review and discuss the findings.

Here are possible open-ended questions for your next, or first, employee-centric culture summit:

- Why do we do (fill in the blank) this way?
- What message are we trying to send with (fill in the blank) policy? How is it and how is it not working?

- What assumptions are baked into (fill in the blank) practice?
- What's the purpose behind our dress code?
- What does 'professional' mean here, and to whom?
- What behaviors are quietly rewarded and punished?
- What work habits might feel outdated to some younger employees?
- What new behavior might feel disrespectful to some older colleagues?
- How does pop culture influence how we show respect or build trust?
- Are we solving a real problem or filling a real need by doing (fill in the blank), or just continuing a tradition?
- What is the best thing about the culture here?
- What is one thing about the company culture that should change? What should it be changed to and why?

Have someone compile and compress the answers. Use the responses as a basis for the summit. Review them in small groups, no larger than 5 people each, asking for feedback.

Have space for articulating additional issues in business practices, from the everyday small issues to the bigger issues.

Holding a yearly organizational employee-centric culture summit is another way to embed a culture of dialogue. If we regularly talk about company and team culture, noticing when something is going off track, issues can be addressed and fixed.

And much more than any one issue being tackled is the feeling employees gain that their real concerns and needs will be regularly listened to and addressed.

What organizational system, policy, procedure, or ritual will you put in place to ensure yearly organizational employee-centric culture summits occur?

Chapter 38: Remember the Goal(s) of Work

For a healthy work environment, all must keep their eye on the prize: What are we doing and why are we doing it?

Next comes the how. How are we going to bring this about? The how will bring about loads of competing ideas, as it should.

We quickly get tricked into majoring on the minors. Our attention gets pulled away from big-picture thinking to going down counter-productive paths when something small is not working for us. Think of how much time and money has been wasted on people being upset about the temperature of the office.

Hold on.

Everyday office issues are important, such as the office temperature. To execute our part in fulfilling the mission of our organization, our physical environment must be addressed.

Place a giant, neon '**yes**' on your do-to list to prioritize the basic human needs of the people on our teams and in our organization. There are right ways and wrong ways to address the basic mechanics of paying attention to our working environment.

The right way to notice, discuss, and decide human-centric policies and procedures is through collaborative dialogue where the goal is to make the environment conducive so everyone can do their best work.

The wrong way to deal with difference is to focus on personalities. To claim that Hank wants the temperature set at 60 degrees because he's selfish, a bully, and cares about no one else, has us focused on Hank's personality instead of the issue at hand.

It is so easy to get pulled into thinking certain behaviors, which we attach to personalities, are of the gravest importance and lose sight of the 'why' of what we are doing at work.

For the health of the organization and your team, which is comprised of people from different generations, consider holding dialogues surrounding the following questions:

- What is the mission of your organization?
- What is the purpose of your department in supporting the organizational mission?
- How, specifically, does your role support your team in advancing its goal to support the mission of the organization?
- What are **your** career goals and overall goals at work?

I imagine 99.99% of the people reading this book have the goal of making money to pay for housing, food, and fun. It is good to be reminded that we (hopefully) want to provide value to others in our jobs and communities, while being reminded of the primary value and good of a regular paycheck.

The reality of the necessity of being gainfully employed should never be left out of these discussions. To provide for yourself, and possibly others, is to be celebrated and thoughtfully protected.

This desire to maintain employment could help temper what we allow to bother us about others at work. It could also cause us to act.

When we are 'bothered,' we tend to think something externally is wrong. We rarely think it's us. When it comes to generation gaps, we are easily tricked into thinking the problem is 'their' way of working and being.

Imagine, if instead of blaming the young, old, or middle aged for what we don't like, we consider the mission and goals of work.

This gives us a path forward to discuss behaviors. Is the behavior you're having a problem with leading away from accomplishing the established mission? Can you explain why?

Now, back to the mundane discussion about office temperature. When we consider the physical working environment as contributing to or taking away from being able to execute the mission of the organization, it is easier to depersonalize it and see it for what it is: an issue to be discussed and solved instead of a personality fight.

With this way of thinking, you are on your way to having a fruitful dialogue instead of eyerolling and stewing in your discontent.

What organizational system, policy, procedure, or ritual will you put in place for all colleagues to know and remember the goals of work?

Section VI: Dialogue in Practice

Chapter 39: Prepare Yourself for a Dialogue

Know Thyself

There are a million books, articles, and videos telling you how to become self-reflective. I will not be able to give you all of the ins and outs of reflective practice here, but I can offer a few important points to consider when getting yourself ready to show up to any dialogue.

- Conflict is about you, and within you.
- Your thoughts about what's important, and any kind of belief in which you've attached a meaning or a judgment, are within your power to reflect on and possibly change.
- What you believe are the motives and reasons behind your colleagues' behavior and what they want is usually wrong, or at least grossly over simplified.

Prepare Thyself

The person you are preparing to have a conversation with is a real person, not a caricature. Having all the right questions, words, and intentions will not be enough if you are unwilling or unable to sit and tolerate personal discomfort.

Holding real conversations with people we don't understand, don't like, or who have caused us pain is hard. Expect some dialogues will be difficult, awkward, or both. Expect it, accept it, and hold those conversations anyway.[67]

Chapter 40: But What If? Barriers to Dialogue

What if my coworker is not interested in having real dialogues?

This is quite possible. Our cultural climate discourages us from holding generous and fruitful conversations with anyone we suspect might disagree with us. What is modeled to us online, in the media, in classrooms, and from our politicians is the opposite of genuine dialogue.

Since this is what you're up against, what are you supposed to do?

Start small. Ask everyday-ordinary professional questions. Get your colleague used to offering input.

Set the conditions for dialogue and normalize it.

What if my coworker is not interested in having real dialogues *with me*?

Get curious. Is it you whom your colleague doesn't want to talk with, or do they not want to talk with anyone?

If you notice it's you, get curious as to why. Could it be your approach, the time and/or location in which you want to hold a dialogue, or a strained dynamic between the two of you?

If you have a good enough working relationship with this colleague, bring it to their attention. You could open with, "I'd like to talk with you about our different approaches to X. Are you open to this discussion?" or "I've felt an unease when the subject of (fill in the blank) is raised. I'd like to talk with you about it."

If you have a trusted mentor or therapist, talk this over with them.

What if my coworker *refuses* to talk to me?

If this unprofessional behavior is being tolerated, there are bigger problems to be addressed before you can get to the good of genuine dialogue.

First, I'd go to your boss to let them know about the situation, assuming you've already tried to talk with your colleague. Your boss may have no idea this is going on.

I suggest you go in with the facts, as you understand them, and not with an emotional plea for help. Consider the difference between:

Anita is the worst! She won't even talk with me! How are we supposed to work together when she constantly gives me the cold shoulder! I just can't take it anymore!

And

I could use your insight and assistance. Anita and I are working on a project together and we are having a hard time communicating. For instance, I asked her three times this week to discuss the project, but it's as if she doesn't hear me. I sent her two emails last week, and a third one this week, and currently she has replied to none. What do you suggest?

But I'm an introvert. Dialogue is for extroverts.

False.

While style preferences of communication differ from person to person and are based on many factors, part of being a professional is developing the ability to have fruitful work-related conversations with colleagues.

Because dialogue is so much more than simple words being exchanged, it's good to know how your colleagues prefer to communicate to maximize the benefits of a real dialogue.

If you struggle with holding dialogues with colleagues, seek out a coach to improve this vital skill.

What if I'm not interested in holding a real dialogue with my coworker, because I simply don't care.

I suppose it depends on the topic of the dialogue. If it's work-related, the fact that you 'don't care' is irrelevant to a large degree. We do tasks at work we don't like or don't care too much about because they simply need to be done. That's part of the gig.

Caring or not caring is dependent on us. If I don't presently care, that is well within my power to change or ignore. Insofar as you want the good of being gainfully employed and maintaining a decent professional reputation, being a good conversation partner is a must.

Well, Merry, I did it. I tried to hold a real dialogue, and it blew up in my face! It didn't work. Thanks for nothing. Now what?

What makes a dialogue successful?

We are tempted to assume a dialogue is a success if our position wins.

However, that is ***not*** what a dialogue is about.

Whenever you hold a dialogue in good faith, you win. You win because you are making progress in developing and refining your conflict capacity, active listening skills, curiosity, and dedication to being a good and competent colleague.

We are not in charge of how anyone else reacts, only our own reactions and responses.

However, let's consider the real concern of "it blew up in my face." I recommend talking to a mentor, conflict coach, Ombuds, therapist, or trusted *non-work* friend to talk through what happened and determine the next steps.

Not all conversations go the way we had hoped, and some of them may feel awful. That's just the way of things. All we can do is show up prepared, be respectful, and make amends whenever we make mistakes.

And we will make mistakes. This is part of the human condition.

What if I don't want to talk to my older/younger coworker because it's painful! The way they talk ... ugh!

I will not gloss over the fact that a sizeable number of people feel this way.

Acknowledge, to yourself, how you feel. Get specific about what is so painful. Is it the tone in their voice, their body language, the words they use, or all the above?

Get specific. Also understand that **if you are annoyed that is a choice you have made.** What great news! This means you can make a different choice. It is within your power to give yourself a different story about your older/younger colleague.

I encourage you to consider all the goods you get professionally and personally from knowing how to be in regular conversations with your colleagues, and all the harm caused when we decide to ignore regular conversations. Considering the benefits and losses, your best option is to deal with your own emotions about the other and hold the conversations. You are damaging yourself and those around you by wallowing in the 'pain' of their age. Choose something better.

I want to hold real dialogues, but I simply lack confidence.

This seems reasonable. To do something difficult, we need confidence. Therefore, if you lack confidence are you out of luck?

Luckily for you that's not the way confidence works. Confidence is gained on the *other side* of the conversation. The experience of preparing and holding a real conversation breeds confidence.

If you think of yourself as conflict avoidant, start small. Begin by developing the skills you need. Practice by yourself, and then practice with a friend. Next, try it out in the office on something minor.

Through the process of holding small, everyday dialogues with colleagues, confidence builds. This is especially the case if you are intentionally working on building your dialogue and conflict capacity.

I don't have time for dialogue. This is work, not a social club.

My dear reader, if this is still your concern, either I've failed, or you haven't paid attention while reading this book.

Regular dialogue saves tons of time and energy.

Regular dialogue is a savvy business strategy that **saves and makes money**.

Regular dialogue at work is not about personal and private matters, but about how to work with your colleagues excellently.

Dialogue is the antidote to unnecessary conflict.

Dialogue is the path forward towards personal empowerment.

Dialogue is the way to win the generation wars at work now and into the future.

End Notes

---

[1] Roosevelt, Eleanor. *Voice of America Broadcast,* November 11, 1951.

[2] Kolbe, Maksymilian Maria. "Prawda." *Rycerz Niepokalanej* 19/20 (December 1940 to January 1941): 6–8.

[3] You may be asking yourself, can you have a conversation with a crowd? The answer is "no."

You can have a town hall meeting, or an open forum where information is exchanged and a large group feels included and seen, but those are not places for dialogue. A real dialogue *could* spring up in a question/answer session in a 10,000 person auditorium where the speaker and question-asker engage in a genuine dialogue, where everyone else in the place falls away, so to speak. But this is the exception.

The highest form of dialogue is found person to person. I and thou. However, this is a book about dialogue at work. These dialogues that center around work expectations and how to treat one another well to bring about healthy work environments need not have the existential weight of a Socratic dialogue.

[4] If you cannot find your way to care about the person you are going to hold a dialogue with, I suggest you refrain. What good would it do?

Real dialogue requires we see our conversation partner as a person who is owed basic respect. If you simply don't care what the other person thinks, or why they think it, a dialogue won't occur.

It is counterproductive to take the attitude of not caring about someone who has a position different from yours. This is like shooting yourself in the foot. Real change requires something of us, and this something is typically difficult. Real dialogue requires (the difficulty of) seeing others as real people with real thoughts, feelings, beliefs, needs, and desires, not as a two-dimensional cardboard cutout.

[5] If you're not sure about the basic kinds of treatment humans as humans deserve, I suggest reading and thinking through the United Nations Universal Declaration of Human Rights (UDHR). This document was written and adopted on December 10, 1949, in the aftermath of the absolute horrors of the Second World War. https://www.un.org/en/about-us/universal-declaration-of-human-rights

[6] A shout out to the importance of everyday, normal, run of the mill, "how's the weather" kinds of conversations at work. While not all conversations rise to the status of a robust and fruitful dialogue, collegial conversations at work create the environment for real dialogue to take place. Most of us have worked in places where everything feels tense, like you're walking on eggshells. Hopefully, most of us have also experienced the opposite of this, where being at work

feels easier in our human interactions, and not rife with tension. Peace to you if you haven't had this kind of work experience.

[7] This might be an odd place to talk about Job from the Old Testament, but it really fits. As a young person, the end of the story of Job never sat well with me. Why are God's words making sense to Job? They don't make sense to me. And then I was introduced to the work of the great American philosopher Eleonore Stump. To (badly) paraphrase her work, there is something that an outsider, like me, to the conversation between Job and God is missing: what it *feels like* to be in this conversation. Job "gets it" because he is there, having the encounter. He's not detached, reading about someone else's experience. It's his experience with the divine. It's living and breathing for him.

When we opt for having real conversations with colleagues, we are present with them. It is the experience of the conversation that can sometimes be just as, if not more, valuable, than the words stated. Being in the presence of people, real people, makes it harder to misunderstand them and makes compassion and caring a whole lot easier.

[8] I also want to make clear that the awful harm and devastation that happens to people because of their treatment at work many times doesn't rise to the level of a crime, at least not currently in the States. Just because it's not a crime, does not lessen the harm.

[9] I am not referring to personal differences and preferences, such as introverted vs. extroverted people. This is about being engaged and welcomed into proper and professional workplace dialogue.

[10] There is a fantastic article about loneliness at work by Constance Noonan Hadley and Sarah L. Wright, published in the Harvard Business Review magazine November-December 2024 edition. "We're Still Lonely at Work." **https://hbr.org/2024/11/were-still-lonely-at-work**

Here are a few more articles to check out:

"Why Encouraging Workplace Friendships Benefits Your Business by Bruce Crumley," Inc., Sept 11,2025. https://www.inc.com/bruce-crumley/why-encouraging-workplace-friendships-benefits-your-busines

"How to Deal With Loneliness At Work by Art Markman, Fast Company," July 27, 2025 https://www.fastcompany.com/91372017/how-to-deal-with-loneliness-at-work

"Employee Loneliness Hurts Your Bottom Line. Here's How to Help by Bruce Crumley," Inc., August 19, 2025. https://www.inc.com/bruce-crumley/employee-loneliness-hurts-your-bottom-line-heres-how-to-help

[11] Are there exceptions to this rule? Sure.

I am now going on a rant you don't have to stay for.

I taught philosophy for over two decades. Whether it's Plato, Augustine, Descartes, Kierkegaard, Marx, or whoever your favorite philosopher is, if they get human nature wrong, their ideas won't work.

I've read a lot of management books. I've seen many organizational structures. The advice and structures that work are the ones rooted in reality, AKA, how humans *really* are, what *really* motivates them, what *really* happens when people are grouped together under a certain set of circumstances.

Get human nature wrong at your peril. Workplaces are populated with people. Real, live people. You MUST get the people piece right for any of the systems to work correctly.

[12] Here is more on the importance of having good relationships at work: https://www.sbam.org/work-besties-the-secret-to-modern-workplace-happiness/

https://www.shrm.org/topics-tools/news/employee-relations/friendship-at-work-boosts-employee-well-being--engagement--and-p

https://wearewildgoose.com/usa/news/workplace-friendship-and-happiness-survey/

[13] Interested in this idea? Here are a few resources: https://bertaux.wordpress.com/wp-content/uploads/2018/04/2013-hbr-how-diversity-can-drive-innovation.pdf

Psychological Safety and Learning Behavior in Work Teams - Amy Edmondson, 1999

https://www.researchgate.net/publication/264334620_Age_diversity_age_discrimination_climate_and_performance_consequences-A_cross_organizational_study

[14] It is important to note that all of us are works in progress. It could be someone (or you) is not willing to collaborate right now, with these people, under these sets of conditions. But the future is not written. Circumstances and people change.

Let's assume that you want to collaborate with colleagues, but you've had terrible experiences working with others in the past. Maybe the thought of collaborating brings back memories of the dreaded school group project. Or maybe you've been mistreated, your ideas have been stollen, you've been walked over, minimized, or not given proper credit for your contributions.

The pains of the past are real.

But that was then. What do you want now? What reputation do you want to build for yourself? What kind of work environment do you want to be a part of?

[15] Interested in setting civility standards for your team but don't know where to start? Reach out to an organization such as mine, Third Party Workplace Conflict Restoration Services. I'm happy to point you in the right direction.

https://www.3pconflictrestoration.com/

[16] When presented with a conflict, do you tend to fight, freeze, flee, or fawn? It's important to be aware of what your go-to reactions are to make progress on responding instead of reacting to situations.

For more on how we react, there are many resources, such as https://www.simplypsychology.org/fight-flight-freeze-fawn.html

[17] Ritualization is one of the best ways to advance the cause of civility and meaningful dialogue. In the context of work, this means having rules that govern behavior, such as Roberts Rules of Order for running a meeting. Some organizations have a designated, physical space in which to hold difficult conversations.

[18] What constitutes misbehaving at work? Talk about it! Discuss it. Align expectations. When you don't, for example, one person's direct mode of communication can be viewed as respectful to those who value directness and disrespectful and aggressive to those who don't.

[19] Consider what our colleagues started out with. Many people's first jobs were in fast food, retail, their family farm, etc. I know not everyone works in corporate America or has (or wants!) a so-called "white collar" job. Also, most of the world does not work in the U.S.

I recommend noting all the ways in which I've gotten this section wrong and set those reasonable concerns to the side to look at the point of this section, which is: think about what you and your colleagues consider normal technology.

[20] Since these are vast generalizations, your experience may be much different. This is worth thinking about.

[21] This section was generation through a conversation between myself and ChatGPT beginning in December of 2024, with modifications made by me.

[22] https://commons.wikimedia.org/wiki/File:A_large_ filled_ rolodex_viewed_from_the_side.jpg

[23] https://upload.wikimedia.org/wikipedia/commons/ 2/24/Emergency_worker_takes_a_nap_in_the_call_center _%2816374226915%29.jpg

[24] https://commons.wikimedia.org/wiki/File:Telefax.JPG

[25] https://commons.wikimedia.org/wiki/File:Students_in_ computer_room,_c1990s_(4359056290).jpg

[26] https://commons.wikimedia.org/wiki/File:Bill_and_ Account_Collectors_-_DPLA_- _8ff14293b72aff6b226ee0c0085d3e7d.jpg

[27] https://commons.wikimedia.org/wiki/File:Posse_ Senadores_2019_(33076008488).jpg

[28] https://commons.wikimedia.org/wiki/File:Technology Hub_2020_Office_Space_Cubicles.jpg

[29] We should all be aware of the difference in treatment that can arise between hourly vs salaried employees. Both can be treated excellently or exploited when it comes to how much is required of them to keep their employment.

[30] A distinction should be made about work inside vs outside the home. The work inside the home is the essential work of keeping us fed, housed, clothed, and (hopefully) loved.

[31] I recommend reading Brummelhuis's article in Forbes, "How To Motivate Gen Z, A Generation That Wants More Work-Life Balance." https://www.forbes.com/sites/lieketenbrummelhuis/2025/05/16/how-to-motivate-gen-z-a-generation-that-wants-more-work-life-balance/

[32] Another way to think of work/life balance is to exchange the word 'balance' for 'blend.' Work/life blend recognizes that there isn't a harsh distinction between our 'working life' and our 'outside of working life.' We think about work at home, and at home we think about work. Thank you to Johnnie Garmon for bringing this word, 'blend,' to this discussion. You can find my conversation with Johnnie on the podcast Conflict Managed, episode 185.

[33] It is certainly the case that loyalty has different meanings for different people. What does it mean to you?

[34] When good employees leave, the organization takes a hit. To name a few, there's the loss in morale felt in their team, productivity, and the significant resources it takes to hire, train, and get new workers up to speed.

This is a great article on how much it really costs to replace someone at work. Employee retention: The real cost of losing an employee: https://www.peoplekeep.com/blog/Employee-Retention-The-Real-Cost-of-Losing-an-Employee#:~:text=%EE%80%80Employee%20turnover%EE%80%81%20occurs

[35] See Chapter 26 in this book for more on this theme.

[36] "The question is often asked, and properly so, in regard to any supposed moral standard – What is its sanction? What are the motives to obey? Or, more specifically, what is the source of its obligation? Whence does it derive its binding force? It is a necessary part of moral philosophy to provide the answer to this question. ... It arises, in fact, whenever a person is called on to *adopt* a standard, or refer morality to any basis on which he has not been accustomed to rest it. For the customary morality, that which education and opinion have consecrated, is the only one which presents itself to the mind with the feeling of *being in* itself obligatory; and when a person is asked to believe that this morality *derives* its obligation from some general principle round which custom has not thrown the same halo, the assertion is to him a paradox...." (J.S. Mill, *Utilitarianism,* chapter III)

[37] Historical Marital Status Tables:
https://www.census.gov/data/tables/time-series/demo/families/marital.html

[38] Tobacco Trends Brief: Overall Tobacco Trends Brief | American Lung Association:
https://www.lung.org/research/trends-in-lung-disease/tobacco-trends-brief/overall-smoking-trends?utm_source=chatgpt.com

[39] Demographics of Mobile Device Ownership and Adoption in the United States:
https://fred.stlouisfed.org/data/ITCELSETSP2USA?utm_source=chatgpt.com

[40] It is important to remember the very nature of belief. What you believe at this moment, you believe is true. Therefore, your current beliefs about how we ought to behave or what is important, you believe are correct beliefs, or you wouldn't hold those beliefs.

This is so simple, and yet we forget. The other people at work, who disagree with you, think they are right, and you are wrong, based on their current set of beliefs, which is based on their current interpretation of the information they have.

This is one of the reasons we need to hold real dialogues. It is in and through the process of the dialogue that we have access to more information. Information, of course, is not limited to cold-hard-facts. The experience of being with and talking with a real-life person, and how that feels, also counts as valuable information.

[41] International shifts in normative differences ought to be addressed. But they won't be in this book.

[42] Gen Z hires are easily offended, and not ready for workplace: business leaders: https://nypost.com/2024/09/14/us-news/gen-z-hires-are-easily-offended-and-not-ready-for-workplace-business-leaders/?utm_source=chatgpt.com

[43] Toxic Expectations & Behaviors Of Old-School Bosses No One Puts Up With Anymore: https://www.yahoo.com/lifestyle/toxic-expectations-behaviors-old-school-141509578.html?guccounter=1

[44] Slang can be found anywhere and isn't exclusive to youth culture. Since this is a book on generational differences, slang is being used here to denote words used by youth with specific youthful meanings.

[45] Take emoji use. First, should they be used in business? It depends on your business.

Second, if emojis are to be used at work, who feels comfortable using them and what do they mean?

For some, emoji use is like looking at a hidden language. Even if you can decipher what the emoji is supposed to mean, pop culture can make it into something entirely different. (I'm looking at you, eggplant emoji.)

I saw a video of a CEO whose favorite emoji was a big grin 😬, or so he thought. After a few months of constantly using the "big grin," one of his employees took pity on him and asked what he thought 😬 meant. He said it was a big smile, because all its teeth are showing. The employee let him know it actually means "grimacing face." This emoji is akin to saying yikes or cringing.

This is similar to the mythical tale of a grandmother who thought 😂 was a sad emoji, using it to spread the word of a death in the family. "Your aunt died last night 😂." But this is not what this emoji means, it means "face with tears of joy."

Of course, depending on when you read this book, these emojis or just about any other word or symbol may have changed meanings.

[46] "Duties as assigned" for the same position differ company to company. They also greatly shift over time. Some workers today remember the secretary pool. It was common for many professionals to have assistants who took dictation, and then typed up letters or memos, sent them out, kept their appointments, screened phone calls, got their coffee and sometimes picked up their dry cleaning.

[47] https://www.snopes.com/fact-check/nobody-wants-to-work-anymore/

[48] New-York Tribune (New York [N.Y.]), September 17, 1882 https://www.loc.gov/resource/sn83030214/1882-0917/ed1/?dl=page&q=younger+generation,+idle&sp=7

[49] The Indianapolis Times (Indianapolis [Ind.]), May 26, 1936, (Final Home Edition, Second Section) https://www.loc.gov/resource/sn82015313/1936-05-26/ed1/?dl=page&q=younger+generation,+idle&sp=14

[50] Lee Adams's lyric "Kids," from the 1960 Broadway musical *Bye Bye Birdie* https://genius.com/Original-broadway-cast-of-bye-bye-birdie-kids-lyrics

[51] "Twentysomething." TIME, 16 July 1990, David M. Gross and Sophfronia Scott. https://time.com/archive/6715389/living-proceeding-with-caution/

[52] Newsweek, "The Whiny Generation," Published Oct 31, 1993 at 7:00 PM EST by Newsweek Staff https://www.newsweek.com/whiny-generation-194042?

[53] By TIME Staff, May 20, 2013 4:40 PM EDT https://time.com/247/millennials-the-me-me-me-generation/

[54] Joel Kotkin, Tue, August 12, 2025 at 12:00 PM CDT

https://www.yahoo.com/lifestyle/articles/young-hipster-socialists-less-screwed-170006013.html

[55] Yes, travel agents still exist.

[56] Let's say you think parking should be free where you work, and you resent having to pay to park there. You can think of no good reason why you should have to pay!

Instead of being stuck in this position, play devil's advocate. Imagine you must come up with reasons why it's reasonable to make workers pay for parking. Maybe it's because:

- Not everyone drives to work, and so those who do drive get a perk that nondrivers don't have.
- It's a standard practice across all businesses in your area, due to the high cost of real estate.
- To maintain the parking lots, they need to be paid for. Since there are a variety of ways to get to work, driving is a chosen way some workers get there, and therefore the service provided by the business (having a parking lot), needs to be, at least in part, paid for by the people who use it.
- Maybe the business wants to encourage use of public transportation or ride sharing.
- Maybe the business owners don't know that this policy of making drivers pay to park is problematic.

Coming up with arguments in defense of views alternative to your position will not necessarily change your mind, but it requires us to stretch, use our imagination, and encourages curiosity.

[57] There are lots of consultants that can take you through the process of determining the right employee-centric values for your team. If you are interested in a workshop to move you through this process, reach out to me and I would be happy to point you in the right direction.

[58] You need an organizational ombuds office! Every company, big, medium or small, needs an ombuds office or access to an outsourced ombuds. The International Ombuds Association is the go-to resource and organization for all things organizational ombuds. If not an organizational ombuds, your employees need access to conflict management professionals. https://www.ombudsassociation.org/

[59] Total side note: aren't we a MILLION TIMES thankful that no one can read our minds! Could you even imagine if your coworker or boss had Edward Cullen's abilities (I see you *Twilight* fans)?

Let me tell you right now, as someone working in the conflict management field – people many times don't know why (or that!) you are upset. They really don't. So, speak up for yourself. It is up to you to find a fruitful path forward with the colleague you are in conflict with. To be clear: I'm talking about the normal, painful things that happen at work, not illegal and immoral activities, such as sexual harassment.

[60] You can find Ronan on Instagram @ronan.thecat.sleeps

[61] Since we are talking about combating generational disconnectedness, I'm focusing on reverse mentoring in regard to age. However, reverse mentoring doesn't need to be tied to age.

[62] A word of caution: talking to one person about their experience and desires and then generalizing to an entire class of people is bad practice. Still, what someone sees as important to them and their friends, and what they've extrapolated out to people in their generation, is helpful information... but always to be taken with a grain of salt. One person's experience and desires are chiefly about that person.

[63] *How to Be Unprofessional at Work: Tips to Ensure Failure* is my book. One of the ways this book has been used, as suggested in this chapter, is by teams reading and thinking through one "tip" a week to set expectations and bring about a healthier work environment. While the book was not written with addressing the generation gap in mind, it is written to facilitate conversation. And as you know, dialogue is the key to winning.

[64] The real pain and harm that people experience at work can be catastrophic. This is not hyperbole.

[65] Understandably, new hires don't want to make enemies. Make this exercise low stakes, so the new hire doesn't feel threatened, but rather as bringing about a meaningful contribution from day one of employment.

Also, keep in mind that the new hire, for many possible reasons, may not have the capacity to offer suggestions or bring up contradictory information.

[66] You can "manage up" by providing basic stats to your manager about how employee retention and engagement improve when the employee-experience is listened to and curated. It will also save your boss lots of time! https://www.themyersbriggs.com/en-US/Company/Newsroom/Press/Press-Releases/2022/Time-Spent-on-Workplace-Conflict-Has-Doubled-Since-2008

[67] This book is an ode to holding difficult conversations at work. While I have mentioned this before, it is worth saying again: you do not owe everyone a conversation. If you are unsure as to whether you should be in dialogue with someone you consider emotionally or physically dangerous, trust your instincts.

It is important to listen to your intuition.

However, sometimes our intuitions are off. For example, if you have practiced avoiding conflict, your instincts might advise you not to have a dialogue that you find difficult. If you know this about yourself, reach out to a mentor or therapist to help you navigate these situations.

Acknowledgements

Thank you to my first reader and editor, Sheila Scott. You have been nothing but wonderful and helpful, catching my typos and being gentle with me and my dyslexic brain.

I am so grateful to my reader friends who have so generously read through this book, offering their time, care, and insights: Dr. Christopher M. Brown, Lisa Smartt, Jeremiah Whiteman, Scott Williams, and Carol Blanchard.

To the many professionals who generously shared their time and expertise on my podcast, Conflict Managed, you have my deepest thanks.

Thank you to my children, Judah, Leo, and Thomas, who have let me practice holding difficult conversations with them. They are the absolute best in the entire world. 🖤

Thank you to my biggest supporter, best friend, and husband, Christopher Brown. Without you, this book would never have seen the light of day. You are the greatest dialogue partner. Thank you for a life full of meaningful conversations.

About the Author

Merry Brown is a writer, speaker, mediator, founder and owner of **Third Party Workplace Conflict Restoration Services**, and host of **Conflict Managed**, a weekly international podcast about toxic work environments and how to fix them.

In addition to "Winning the Generation Wars At Work: Making (Your) Age An Asset," she is the author of "How to Be Unprofessional at Work: Tips to Ensure Failure," "The Food Addict: Recovering from Binge Eating Disorder & Making Peace with Food" as well as two young adult series, featuring "The Knowers" and "Gold Manor Ghost House."

Connect with Merry Brown

Email: 3pconflictrestoration@gmail.com
Website: 3pconflictrestoration.com
LinkedIn: linkedin.com/in/merry-brown
TikTok: @3pconflictrestoriation
Conflict Managed is available wherever you listen to podcasts and to watch on YouTube @3pconflictrestoration